BITTER
MEDICINE

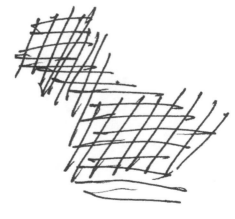

Bitter Medicine

A Graphic Memoir of Mental Illness

Clem Martini and Olivier Martini

Freehand Books gratefully acknowledges the support of the Canada Council for the Arts for its publishing program. ¶ Freehand Books, an imprint of Broadview Press Inc., acknowledges the financial support for its publishing program provided by the Government of Canada through the Book Publishing Industry Development Program (BPIDP).

Canada Council Conseil des Arts
for the Arts   du Canada

Library and Archives Canada Cataloguing in Publication

Martini, Clem, 1956–
Bitter medicine : a graphic memoir of mental illness / Clem Martini and Olivier Martini.

Includes bibliographical references.
ISBN 978-1-55481-114-4

1. Martini, Ben—Mental health.
2. Martini, Olivier—Mental health.
3. Schizophrenics—Family relationships.
4. Mental health services—Alberta.
5. Schizophrenics—Canada—Biography.
I. Martini, Olivier.
II. Title.

RC514.M359 2010   616.89'800922   C2009-907035-9

Edited by Melanie Little
Cover and interior design by Natalie Olsen, www.kisscutdesign.com

Freehand Books
515 – 815 1st Street SW
Calgary, Alberta T2P 1N3
www.freehand-books.com

Book orders
Broadview Press Inc.
280 Perry Street, Unit 5
Peterborough, Ontario K9J 7H5
Phone: 705-743-8990
Fax: 705-743-8353
customerservice@broadviewpress.com
www.broadviewpress.com

Printed on FSC recycled paper and bound in Canada

To our family: immediate, extended, alive, and dead.

And to all those who live and struggle with mental illness.

Office of the President

COMMON READING | UNIVERSITY OF
PROGRAM | **CALGARY**
2012 SELECTION

Welcome to the University of Calgary! You've chosen to join a talented, driven and accomplished community of students, faculty and staff, and I am confident your experience here will be filled with challenges, excitement and discovery.

Your very first assignment will be to participate in the Common Reading Program, our community book club. Every new undergraduate student will be provided with the 2012 selection, *Bitter Medicine: A Graphic Memoir of Mental Illness*, and will be invited to participate in an online forum to discuss the book with other students, faculty and staff. A highlight of the program will be the opportunity to hear the book's authors, Clem and Olivier Martini, address students at our annual New Student Induction Ceremony during Fall Orientation Week.

Bitter Medicine was chosen by a committee of faculty, staff and students and is a brave account of an issue that touches us all. This book challenges stereotypes and preconceived notions about mental illness, and is an invitation to develop new perspectives. It is our hope that by participating in the Common Reading Program and Fall Orientation Week, you will reflect on your role as a student and a citizen, and be inspired to think critically and to tackle pressing issues facing society today.

The University of Calgary is committed to equipping our students with the skills and the knowledge they need by fostering their talents, and in particular, to nurturing leadership ability. The Common Reading Program is our unique and creative invitation to you to explore your potential, and I encourage you to embrace the opportunity to participate.

We welcome you to our community.

Sincerely,

Elizabeth Cannon
President
University of Calgary

Introduction

A lot has been written about mental illness from a clinical perspective, but very little attempts to truly understand the experience from within and across a family. In *Bitter Medicine*, my brother Olivier and I have tried to do that: to generate some kind of understanding by tossing questions back and forth and chewing them over, me with words, my brother with drawings. It's been more than three decades since our younger brother was first diagnosed. I imagine we've spent the better part of those past thirty years, each in our own manner, reviewing and chewing.

Many of the remembrances raised and discussed in this process were awkward, painful, and private, things we often would have preferred to avoid or ignore. I hope that in writing and drawing our way through this, we've managed to capture some element of the truth.

A parallel world exists beyond the one we normally operate in. This is the story of how my family entered that other dimension and has never been able to fully return.

Clem Martini and Olivier Martini
Calgary, Alberta, July 2009

Part One

The biggest thing to understand is that we were nothing remarkable.

We were four skinny boys with bad haircuts growing up in a tiny grey house perched near the foothills. The town we lived in was small and, in the summer months, laden with dust. There were only gravel roads then, and one lonely street lamp down at the end of the corner that flickered and writhed when thunderstorms swept through. Bowness hadn't yet been swallowed and digested by our neighbouring community, Calgary. It still required two buses and a transfer if you wanted to perform any kind of serious shopping.

We owned a restless black spaniel, a fat, white short-haired rabbit, and a cat that was grey as a puff of smoke. (A little poetic perhaps, but that's the way I thought of her. Everyone smoked back then, so I suppose it was only natural.) We didn't have much money, so during the hot, dry summers we camped down in the badlands and hiked to pass the time. We took turns climbing among the sun-baked hills with the dog. We searched for the glossy, serrated dinosaur teeth that could be found glittering among the clay and cacti and the massive, rusty stumps of petrified wood.

When the temperature rose, we retreated to our tattered canvas tent to read worn paperback novels we'd picked up for twenty-five cents apiece from the everything-must-go bin at the used bookstore. When it grew too hot to read even bad science fiction, we'd cast the books aside, slip on our baggy army surplus trunks, and wade chest-deep in the muddy current of the Red Deer River.

WE WENT TO DRUMHELLER AND DINOSAUR PARK

I thought I had our future lives mapped out. Liv, my second oldest brother, unearthed more dinosaur bones than anyone else. From this evidence I concluded that he was destined to become a paleontologist. (Though he was also the only one among us who had discovered flint arrowheads on several occasions, so there was, I assumed, the outside chance he would become an archaeologist.) Nic, the eldest and our undisputed leader, could identify every tree, bush, or cactus from a single seed or needle. He would, I was certain, secure employment as one of those park naturalists my family so admired.

I wanted to write. I wasn't sure where you applied for a job like that, though, or what credentials were required. I thought maybe I'd work in a zoo instead. I liked animals.

OUR DOG ATE GARBAGE
WE COULDN'T TRAIN HIM

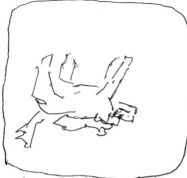

OUR DOG ROLLED
IN DEAD FISH OR
COWPIES

WE HAD A RABBIT
NAMED NOSEY

NOSEY DIED

WE BURNED HIM
UP IN OUR BURNING
BARREL

MOM TOLD ME
NOSEY WAS OLD

Ben was the youngest and the smartest of us four. He was, without doubt, the best looking. While I didn't know what he was going to be exactly, I was pretty sure it would be good. He was the golden boy. Total strangers commented on how cute he was, how clever, how destined for big things. The rest of us tended toward being too bony, too gangly, and we were cursed with my dad's long, aquiline nose. Ben somehow got the short-nose gene. We were all short-sighted. Back then that meant you strapped on glasses constructed of two thick oblong lenses attached to a frame made of a kind of black acrylic girder. Ben didn't receive his prescription until glasses were fashionably rimmed with thin silver wire.

Taken as a package, though, we were pretty average. Nobody spent any time thinking about us.

ONE DAY WE HAD MICE

MOM BOUGHT A
CAT

FRIGIDAIRE

MY DAD CLOSED
THE DOOR OFTHE
REFRIGERATOR
ON THE CAT
BECAUSE HE
THOUGHT IT WAS
A MOUSE

THE CAT WAS BURNED
UP IN THE BURNING
BARREL

OUR HOUSE HAD A
PUMP AND A WELL

NIC AND I TOOK
BATHS IN A TUB IN
THE KITCHEN. MOM
AND DAD HEATED
WATER ON THE STOVE

ONE DAY THE PUMP
WENT DRY

MY MOM WAS PREGNANT
AND WENT DOWN
THE WELL

MY MOM WENT INTO
THE WELL BUT
COULD NOT GET
OUT

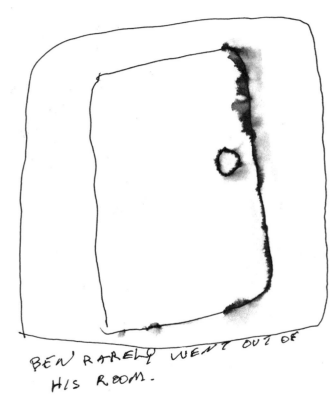

BEN RARELY WENT OUT OF
HIS ROOM.

The summer Ben graduated from high school he didn't do much of anything. He said he was pursuing job applications but rarely left the house. He stayed in his bedroom with the lights turned off. Whatever you asked him to do, he couldn't. He slept excessively, and when he woke he was irritable. We took this to mean he was anxious about finding work.

Things quickly went sideways from there. He started picking arguments, particularly with Liv. He refused to come to dinner. His testiness put everyone on edge. One afternoon I confronted him. What was going on? I asked. Instead of responding angrily, he surprised me by confiding that he wasn't feeling right.

What did that mean? I asked. He didn't know but said that it felt strange. I advised him to see a counsellor. He made me promise not to tell anyone about what he'd shared with me. He said he wanted to try to work it out on his own.

A few nights later, at three a.m., a quiet knock at my door woke me. Ben entered and sat at the foot of my bed. I turned on my bedside lamp. In his arms he carried three objects. A carefully folded tissue. A pair of wire-rim glasses. A stack of thick books.

This was proof, he told me. Here was evidence of something new and strange.

He had been approached, he told me, by someone from another world. A hand had reached across dimensions and deposited a thumbprint on the lens of his glasses. He shoved the frames across the bed to me. A smudge clouded the right lens.

A scratch had appeared upon the surface of the lens as well, he informed me, and he had peeled it off as though it was a dried scar. That scab he had wrapped in the tissue. He handed it to me gently. I held it and felt my heart begin to race. What did he expect me to do with it? I asked.

Take it to a drugstore and have it analyzed, he told me.

He turned his attention to the books. These texts, he said, patting them gingerly, spoke to him. They tried to control his life, and unless he stacked them in a particular order they gave him commands.

The quiet of the night seemed to grow louder. I suggested that he seek some kind of help. His face crumpled. This, he insisted, wasn't fantasy. This was *real*.

We argued back and forth through the night. At six a.m. I rose to get ready for work. You've got to see someone, I begged Ben for the last time. He picked his things up and left the room. "It's all been for nothing," he muttered and closed the door.

No chaos quite matches the confusion that accompanies trying to check someone into the hospital for psychiatric assessment. If he doesn't want to go, what are your options?

Compelling someone to take an examination is difficult. The law requires that you prove the individual in question is a danger to himself or to others, but how exactly is that accomplished? In Ben's case, discussing it with him was out of the question. He just got angry. He leapt out the passenger door of a moving car when Mom tried to drive him to a psychiatric appointment.

Months passed as we struggled to figure it out. A heavy silence hung over our house. We met like conspirators. We'd collect after dark at the local bar so that Ben wouldn't hear us talking.

If he'd felt paranoid before, now he had his reasons. He smelled something in the wind. He paced the hallways between midnight and four a.m. One afternoon in late fall an argument between Ben and Liv became a shouting match and then a shoving match. Suddenly, Ben knocked everyone aside and flew out our front door. When my older brothers tried to fetch him, a fist fight broke out down by the train tracks. Ben slipped from Nic's grasp, scrambled down the gravel embankment, and hid in the dense brush by the river.

MOM MADE A CALL TO
THE POLICE.

THE POLICE CAME

THE POLICE SEARCHED
FOR DRUGS

THEY TOOK BEN AWAY

It was an especially bitter November. Snow fell that night and the temperature dropped to -30° C. When Ben returned home the next day, he'd frozen his nose, his toes, and his fingertips. He glared at us, slouched into his bedroom without a word, and drew the door shut.

My mother disappeared into her bedroom and made a muffled phone call. A police car pulled into our driveway. Two uniformed officers entered our house. One stood by the bedroom door, the other snapped cuffs on Ben's wrists. Together they escorted him out to the squad car.

So this is how it's done, I thought.

BEN WAVED HIS HANDS
IN THE AIR.

MOM TRIED TO PUT
BEN IN HOSPITAL

BEN WOULD RUN
AWAY AT NIGHT
IT WAS MINUS 30
OUTSIDE

Things are supposed to improve when you bring someone to the hospital—but they didn't. The fog we were under didn't lift. Instead it sank lower, became denser. A diagnosis was slow in coming. Ben remained uncooperative. He stopped talking entirely: to us, to the doctors. After a few days he slipped past a psychiatric attendant and out the door, running from the hospital dressed only in his flimsy hospital gown and slippers. He made his way as far as the main highway, where he was captured and fetched back.

He waited for his opportunity and ran again.

BEN WOULD RUN
AWAY FROM THE
FOOTHILLS. I REMEMBER
GOING TO SUPERS DRUGS

MOM PICKED HIM UP
AT SUPERS.

HE WORE ONLY A GOWN
FROM THE FOOTHILLS HOSPITAL

The family visited but that didn't prove very productive. Ben stayed angry and ignored us. Quite frankly, so did the medical staff. Ignore us, that is. I didn't understand their behaviour then, and it wasn't until some years later that I began to appreciate that this was a way of engaging with the world that's systemic to psychiatric units. If you've never visited a psychiatric ward, you have to realize that the environment is like nowhere else. Patients shuffle through the hallways, moan or murmur to themselves or repeat the same question over and over. The staff, seated behind the front desk, learn—to an extent—to tune these surroundings out. That tuning out grows over time to extend to visitors as well. Our questions about treatment were briefly noted and just as quickly forgotten.

Once Ben had been admitted to their care, it was hard not to feel like a nuisance with our endless queries and concerns.

The staff increased Ben's medication and he finally abandoned his energetic attempts to escape. Instead he sprawled impassively on his bed. I would sit in his tiny room and stare as he stretched out on his cot, studiously ignoring me. I felt depressed. Lost. We were all tired, I realized. Between arguing and chasing and fighting and worrying, the entire family was drained. Medicate us all, I wanted to tell the nurses. Give us whatever you've given him, and a dark room to lie down in. We all need to recover. Maybe a long sleep will do the trick.

The diagnosis, once delivered, produced more confusion than clarity.

Like everyone else, I knew little about schizophrenia. A disorder of the brain, they told us. It could generate hallucinations, both visual and aural, paranoid behaviour, passivity, and confusion.

There was no certainty about what caused it. There wasn't any cure. It could surface early in one's life, or late. Maybe it was caused by a virus. Maybe it was genetic. Some who developed it could, with treatment, lead independent lives. Some, with treatment, were able to diminish the worst impact but led lives requiring considerable medical support and attention. Some never stopped hallucinating, never recovered, and instead became catatonic, or increasingly violent, or so fearful and delusional that they remained unable to cope or respond to treatment and required permanent institutionalization.

The suggested treatments took some getting used to. In some ways they seemed hardly better than the disorder. Insulin therapy, for instance: administer insulin until the patient experiences a minor coma. Hope that when the patient recovers, his brain will have shed the disturbance. Shock therapy: administer a sizzling electric current to the brain to induce a remedial, cleansing seizure.

Mostly, though, the recommended treatment was pharmaceutical, and that meant regularly administered, powerful drugs. For some people, that seems like a bad thing, but it's important to remember that prior to the advent of drug treatments individuals diagnosed with schizophrenia were simply collected and warehoused in enormous segregated wards. Once there, they tended to remain locked in for the rest of their lives. The living conditions were, by and large, grim.

The advent of antipsychotic drugs liberated psychiatric patients. Many were able to shed the majority of the most disabling symptoms and live something approaching an independent life. Certainly, that was our hope for Ben.

But there were side effects. Dry mouth. Uncontrollable shaking. Severe inner restlessness that manifested itself with the inability to sit still or remain motionless. A kind of physical twitching. Neuroleptic Malignant Syndrome, a life-threatening neurological disorder caused by severe reaction to the drugs and manifested by fever, delirium, and muscle rigidity.

Ben took his drugs, shed his hallucinations, gained weight, and watched his body stiffen by degrees.

I REMEMBER BEN CROSSING ACROSS A CREEK. HE HAD TROUBLE BECAUSE HIS MEDICATION MADE HIM RIGID

Justification is one tiny ingredient of a vast cocktail you imbibe when mental illness is introduced to your life. You find yourself justifying everything. You justify what you attend to and what you ignore. Here is how I justified leaving the country.

I felt I had been consumed by the experience of first identifying Ben's mental illness and then somehow arranging that he receive treatment at a hospital. I felt betrayed, if not by Ben, then by life. Something had stolen my younger brother and mysteriously replaced him with a complete stranger. I felt rejected, by Ben and by the health care system. There seemed to be no place in the process for me. The doctors and the nurses informed us that there was little we could do to help, that it was best if we didn't interfere.

At times it was even implied that perhaps we had done something of harm. (This ideology proved particularly hurtful for my mother, who wondered what she could possibly have done. There were, back then, those in the field of psychology who believed that schizophrenia was potentially generated by unhealthy parenting. That, thankfully, has been almost entirely discredited. Schizophrenia remains a remarkably democratic disorder, making its appearance among families of all kinds.) In any case, we were all impotent. Beside the point.

I needed time to put things into perspective, I told myself. I needed a change. Ben seemed so totally in a fury at me, at what he regarded as my betrayal of his confidence, that we hardly talked anyway. How helpful could my visits be at this point? It was more painful than therapeutic whenever I visited him in the psychiatric ward.

And I reasoned that he could probably use a break from me. As tired as I was of hospitals, psychiatrists, and the enveloping lack of clarity, he must, I felt, be equally tired of me. In the end, I thought that it would be good for both of us if I left.

I purchased an airplane ticket to Europe and informed Ben on my subsequent visit that I was going on a trip. He looked up blearily through a fog of medication and said that he would probably never see me again. I assured him he would and that I would return within a few months, but he studiously ignored my reply.

Once in Europe, I felt consumed again. This time by guilt. Late one evening while I was in Paris I dialled home from a pay phone. By then Ben had been released from the hospital. As an outpatient, he returned weekly to the hospital's clinic to receive his medication and attend group therapy. The telephone connection was dreadful. Bursts of unexpected static interrupted and from time to time snatches of other conversations, distant and ghostly, intruded. I shouted to Ben over the crackle that I would be on my way home soon.

IT RAINED THE DAY
OF THE FUNERAL

I received an unexpected telegram when I reached
Strasbourg, delivered to the apartment of a friend,
telling me to call home. The friend I was staying
with didn't own a phone, but she guided me along
the canals to the post office where I could place
a call. Inside the crumbling government building,
an old-fashioned bank of phone booths was clus-
tered in the corner. I waited in a winding queue
of mostly young foreigners like myself. Eventually,
I took a ticket from a bored attendant, entered a
booth, and dialled the number.

This time the connection was much better.
Everything was perfectly clear. My mother greeted
me, paused as though searching for the correct
way to begin, then simply said, "Come home.
Your brother is dead."

MY BROTHER BEN WAS
SICK

THEN HE GOT
A GUN

BEN TOLD ME HE WANTED
TO SHOOT GOPHERS

This, I learned, was how things unfolded.

Ben disappeared one day. He didn't show up at his group therapy at the appointed time and he didn't return home later for supper. No one knew where he had gone. Eventually, my mother grew worried and phoned his friends. No one could provide information about where he might have gone. Then one friend admitted that he had recently lent Ben money to purchase a rifle. To shoot gophers, he explained.

My mother hung up and phoned my two older brothers. Ben hadn't returned home, she told them. It seemed he had purchased a gun. She threw on a coat and went out looking for him.

I SHOULD HAVE SEEN IT
COMING

My father descended into the basement to see whether Ben had left a note. A tiny storage area was unlit, the overhead light burned out. Stacks of old books and magazines rose from the floor, forming a kind of teetering partition. My father entered that darkness, stepped around the books, and found Ben's body, still seated in the corner, still holding the gun.

Suicide and schizophrenia are intimately related.

According to the Canadian federal government's latest findings on the status of mental health, suicide is one of the leading causes of death among people with schizophrenia. More than 40 percent will attempt suicide at least once. Males top the list: approximately 60 percent will make at least one attempt. The overall result is that 10 to 15 percent of those with schizophrenia die at their own hands. That's a conservative estimate. Many suicides go unreported.

That rate of mortality makes schizophrenia one of the deadlier diseases you'll ever encounter. Nobody ever tells you that.

The first six to nine months after people with
schizophrenia are released from hospital are,
statistically speaking, some of the worst. That's
when a good portion kill themselves. That's when
the medication has had sufficient time to really
kick in. The delusions disappear and people are
able to see, really see with a kind of lucidity for
the first time, the true scope of their illness. How
lifelong a struggle it will be.

If they can make it through those first critical
months, they can develop other skills, find a new
community to compensate for the one they've
lost, develop alternate support systems. But in that
initial intense burst of brilliant, blinding clarity, it
all can feel too demanding, too discouraging, too
overwhelming.

Ben and I had been close friends. He was my partner in nearly every childhood activity. His sudden departure sucked the air out of me. I arrived home after the funeral, and it was as though he had been erased from my life. Everything proceeded as before, only in those tens of thousands of instances where he would have appeared and played a vital role, he didn't.

Suicide provides such a rich vein of shame that it is almost inexhaustible for the mining. Everything reminds you of what you might have done, or failed to do. Normally after a funeral, the community provides support. That's not the way things roll after a suicide. The small kindnesses one usually encounters after a family member dies are almost entirely absent following a suicide. People are so frightened, embarrassed, or anxious that they stay away. They don't phone and they don't stop by. It's hard not to conclude that you are being shunned.

My family became nearly invisible in the community, and in a sense, we became invisible even to ourselves. My father spent his days in long, solitary walks. My mother attended business conferences out of town. My brothers returned to their respective workplaces. I immersed myself in theatre studies at university.

We didn't talk about Ben. What was there to talk about?

And yet, you do. Talk. You hold conversations with yourself.

As you prepare for sleep, you pose the same questions. You feel exhausted when you wake. You don't share your hurt with anyone because you know that everyone else is struggling as well. Why burden others?

My mother wrestled with feelings of guilt. She had always been an outgoing person, very capable and articulate. Now, struck by her own sense of inadequacy, she retreated.

My father took the madness and death as a personal failure. A failure of foresight. A failure of support. A failure of his genetics, something in his very makeup that had betrayed him and contributed to the death of his youngest son. For him, talking about it with outsiders was unthinkable. This was the most private of family matters.

Reactions from the community slowly filtered back to us. Sympathy cards were deposited in the mail. One lady took the time to craft and send a painstakingly detailed letter, exhorting us to return to the church, warning us that Ben roasted in Hell as a result of his mortal sin. She didn't bother signing her last name or leaving a return address.

Some old high school acquaintances conspired to cheer me up. They arrived at my home unexpectedly, lifted me over our front-yard fence, and hauled me out to get drunk. At the bar, one of them patted me on the back and told me not to blame myself. He leaned in close and confided with a boozy, quiet authority that he'd heard from good sources that Ben had been hooked on illicit drugs for some time. That's what had made him crazy and had driven him to kill himself. I stared at him and listened, over the voices and the western band and the general din of the bar. On what basis, I wondered, did he possibly feel qualified to tell me this? And why did he expect that this information would make me feel better?

I excused myself, left the bar, and wandered home down empty streets. As I walked, I reflected on the myths and fairy tales that had been invented to make sense of my brother's death.

I can remember, quite clearly, rounding the corner of 34th Avenue, suddenly seeing our old grey house looming out of the darkness and thinking that when I arrived I would still find Ben there. I was that certain that I had dreamt it all.

Part Two

Ben's bedroom remained largely untouched, the books he'd last read on their shelves gathering dust, his clothes still hanging in the closet. It stayed that way until my mother sold the house and moved decades later.

In the meantime, Nic got married. Liv returned to Calgary after leaving his employment in Olds and found work in the print shop at the University of Calgary. I graduated and moved to Montreal to study playwriting at the National Theatre School.

It was three a.m. a few months into my first semester, and I was asleep in my apartment when I received a phone call. My girlfriend, Cheryl, upset by a conversation she'd had earlier and unable to sleep, called to tell me that something was wrong. She had been talking with Liv, and he had told her that he had seen mysterious white vans tailing his car, people abducted, the FBI following him home. Cheryl told me she was worried, that it all felt too scarily familiar to her.

I hung up the phone and thought back to Ben. Everything bad happens at three a.m.

I phoned Olivier the next day and asked what was going on. He laid it out for me. Someone had been kidnapped. The television was sending him signals. He was being followed. There was a conspiracy.

I interrupted him and asked whether he felt these thoughts were normal. No, he answered hesitantly, but that didn't mean they weren't real. Shouldn't he seek some help? I asked. He considered this question for a long time and finally answered that he was too frightened. Frightened he'd be abducted, frightened that "they" would do something.

This placed us at an impasse. We turned things over for some time but didn't seem to make any progress. Finally, I asked if he would fly out to visit me. Perhaps together we could figure things out. He had accumulated some overtime at work and I think he probably welcomed an opportunity for a break of some kind. He replied that a visit might be a good idea.

I hung up the phone and glanced out the window of my third-floor apartment on Aylmer in the McGill Ghetto. It offered me a crystal-clear view of the future. This is how it looked. I could see Liv initially resisting treatment. I could see him ultimately checking into a psychiatric hospital anyway at my urging. There, the medical authorities would diagnose him, treat him, release him, and, when he was ready, permit him to kill himself. The end.

I closed the blinds, sat in a chair in my kitchen, and made a list of things I would do differently this time.

Liv arrived at the Montreal airport, and I could tell as he descended the escalator to the luggage pickup area how deeply in trouble we were. He was happy to see me, but his expression was withdrawn, as though he were dealing with things of greater consequence inside his head. As we took the bus to my apartment, I saw him cast worried glances at people in nearby seats.

My apartment was cramped, squalid, and littered with books, but Liv found the compact space surprisingly comforting. For the entire time he visited me, he refused to leave unless I accompanied him. He would sit on my lumpy, lopsided sofa throughout the day, maybe reading, maybe thinking, until I returned after classes. Then, as I turned the key in the lock, he would call anxiously through the door, "Is that you, Clem?"

I soon discovered that when we left the apartment to go to a restaurant, or when we took the subway, he saw things I didn't. On one trip he asked me whether I had noticed the people behind us putting on masks.

Liv wasn't Ben, though.

Ben would get frustrated and then angry if you contradicted his visions. Liv, as he grew distressed, retreated into himself. When I urged him to see someone, he became quieter and quieter. Though the silence made things awkward, at last we reached an agreement.

We would use the time until Christmas as an exploration. He would see whether he was feeling better—or, if he found he wasn't feeling better, he would seek professional help. If, by Christmas, he was neither feeling better nor had been able to seek assistance, he and I would go to a clinic together.

I consulted the calendar. The holidays were only a month away.

I returned home to a cold Christmas. Snow layered the streets and ice fog billowed in the air. Inside my family's house, the Christmas decorations had been set out, but the conversation was muted. We followed the rituals of celebration without any genuine celebration. There seemed to be so many things that couldn't be talked about.

Then, on my third night back, I walked into the living room. It was dark except for the Christmas tree, which shimmered in a corner. Several of its bulbs were old-fashioned, containing a kind of caramelized, coloured liquid that bubbled as the lights grew hotter; the shadows in the room swirled and crawled. Liv sat near the tree, on the couch, and in the dim, shifting light I thought I could see him crying. I asked him what the trouble was. He answered that he had taken a walk to the river and tried to kill himself but couldn't seem to get it right.

I suggested that it was time that we went to the hospital. He agreed, and together we packed a small, battered backpack. Then we walked out to the car and drove through the snow and, for the second time in my life, a brother of mine passed intake at the psychiatric ward.

Part Three

Taking someone to the hospital for a psychiatric assessment is never easy, and it's never *made* any easier either.

The mechanism for bringing someone in and registering him for a psychiatric assessment isn't clear. As many times as you perform it, you always feel perplexed, awkward, and in the way. And there's no certainty that after that initial conversation with the medical personnel you will ever be listened to or consulted again. As soon as your family member is checked in, you become dispensable.

It may be because the hospital staff feel the need to attend to the concerns of the patient. Maybe it's because the caseloads are so heavy. Perhaps there is a concern for the confidentiality of clients.

In any case, it's just that way.

I SAT IN MY
ROOM W'IN THE DARK

WHEN I WENT TO
UNIT 49 I SAT IN
MY ROOM WITH THE
LIGHTS OFF

ONE OF THE NURSES CAME AND
SAID MAYBE IT WOULD BE
BETTER IF I WENT
OUT SIDE OF MY ROOM

I should spend a moment describing psychiatric wards in greater detail. Literature presents two conflicting visions, both obsolete (if there was ever any truth to them). One is a kind of desperate portrait of bedlam. Miserable patients kill time, wrapped in filthy gowns. Dour doctors and severe-looking attendants roam the hallways. It's gothic, grim, scary.

The other portrait presents a more comic vision of a world turned upside down. The wards are inhabited by individualists and iconoclasts of all kinds. Patients play cards and exchange conversations redolent in a kind of pithy, alternative wisdom. In this version, doctors and attendants are occasionally frustrated by the patients but nevertheless indulgently amused. There's a lot of wry laughter.

In my experience, psychiatric wards have never been a lot of laughs.

Physically, they aren't much different from any of the other hospital units. There is perhaps a greater informality than you might encounter elsewhere in the hospital. You'll find a largish room where a scattering of tattered, out-of-date magazines and loosely stacked newspapers can be assembled to be read. In that same general vicinity you'll notice jigsaw puzzles in various states of completion. Several shelves will contain old board games and an assortment of the previous decade's lesser known films. Near reception there'll be a common area where friends and visitors can sit with patients and some smaller alcoves where people can discuss matters more privately.

I PACED BACK AND
FORTH ON M2

OUR NURSE FOR THE DAY
WAS LISTED ON A WHITE
BOARD. I THOUGHT THE NAMES
WERE FAKE SO WE NEVER KNEW

But you'll be required to buzz the front desk before receiving permission to enter, and the door will close with a loud click, locking behind you.

A patient in a hospital gown may stand gazing at nothing in particular. At the front desk someone may admonish another patient to step away from the entrance. Frequently you'll hear someone, somewhere, crying.

You may be greeted, as I was in one ward, by a gaunt young man who bowed deeply from the waist. Each visit, as I proceeded to Liv's room, he kept a steady, reversed pace with me, walking backwards step for step, bowing, pleading urgently in a language I couldn't understand.

Or you may find yourself confronted, as I was in another ward, by an ancient lady who grasped my hand earnestly and requested that I "Come this way, dear. Come this way." Initially we wound through the hallways until it became clear that she had not the slightest idea where she was taking me or why.

Somewhere on the ward a patient will perform some kind of ritualized behaviour. In one ward a thin young man paced a series of complicated geometrical figures again and again through the common area. In another, an older man stood patiently polishing his bald head with the pyjama sleeve of his right arm.

And presiding over this will be the front desk, staffed by nurses and attendants who look tired, distant, and busy.

I WENT TO INTENSIVE
FEELINGS GROUP

I CRIED ALMOST
EVERY DAY IN
FEELINGS GROUP.

In other wards at the hospital you'll experience an atmosphere of urgency and purpose.
The prevailing sensations upon walking into
a psychiatric ward are of sadness, failure, and
shame. Unlike in any other ward at the hospital,
there is a feeling that this illness is *someone's*
fault. And oddly, there is also a lingering sense of
confusion. Those at the desk will resist diagnosing
the ailment. Nobody will be able to tell you how
long treatment will take, nor what treatment may
involve. The front desk staff will either not have
the precise information you require or will be
forbidden to release it.

It occurs to me that, because I'm writing these words, my role sounds larger than it really was. All you can ever do is express your own particular perspective, but the reality is that families are a team sport. Sometimes you are on the court; other times you are seated on the bench. As I've noted, I was away a lot of the time. My family struggled, as all families do, with how to handle each moment of every day of a very complicated situation. And Liv, situated as he was in the centre, struggled the hardest. That he sought help, got help, and was open to applying that help is a credit to him. That he was able to stay the course and maintain his treatment was due largely to the many attributes he possesses. He is by nature quiet and shy, but what he knows about commitment, dedication, and determination can't be taught.

If I also make events sound universally grim, I should point out that wasn't always the case. There were good and bad days. Some were a curious mixture of both, with a generous portion of the surreal.

For instance, only a day after Liv had gone through intake for the first time, I ran a few errands and then returned to my parents' home. I don't remember whether I was humming to myself, but I might have been. I was in that sort of mood. There's an odd feeling of extreme calm that descends upon you after you have taken someone to the hospital. So much confusion and anxiety precedes that visit, so much hasty, intense emotional communication and tortured self-scrutiny, that when you finally arrive at your decision and act upon it, everything goes very quiet. Stripped of the turmoil, purged of your present troubles, the world suddenly feels simple and serene.

So when I returned to my parents' house and saw that Liv was sitting on the sofa, I was completely stunned. I abruptly thought back to the number of times Ben had escaped from the hospital. How fiercely he had wanted out. How angry he'd been. I wondered whether I had the strength to argue with Liv.

I sat and asked what had happened. He replied that he had taken his medication, as instructed. Not appearing to have anything else to add, he grew silent and glanced out the window.

Right, I said and encouraged him to go on. Well, he continued, then he sat on the ward for several hours. The psychiatric attendants didn't seem to expect anything else from him. The doctors didn't seem to expect anything else from him. He had gone in for observation, and they'd certainly *observed* him. So...

"So?" I repeated, still hoping he would tell me why he was here.

So, he told me, he figured they didn't need him anymore. He had quietly gathered his things together, got dressed, and slipped out the front door. He strolled along the riverbank for the six or so miles until he arrived home.

I digested that. Okay, I told him, I could see the logic in his decision. But, I suggested, they might want to *observe* him a little longer. I was sure they meant, I continued, for him to stay for *several weeks* of observation. He thought about that a moment, then said, "Oh. All right." And he stood up to go. Just like that. No argument.

I believe he would have walked back the way he had come if I hadn't offered him a ride.

74

Life slips into suspended animation when a family member checks into a psychiatric ward. You all, collectively, hold your breath. Major decisions are placed in limbo until you determine how successful treatment will be.

I had graduated from the National Theatre School by this time and returned to Calgary. I rented a small apartment, settled in, and helped out where I could. The family's day-to-day schedule became regulated by the rhythms of hospital routine. Everyone took turns visiting. We consulted one another about who was to bring clean clothes. Who would fetch the mail? Who would transport the Tupperware-sealed pieces of chocolate cake following birthday celebrations?

In our conversations with Liv, we tried to stay positive. Tried not to talk about anything too serious, or too provoking, or too private. There were always patients who didn't receive visitors and they would edge close and attempt to listen in.

Liv remained subdued. He told me he attended the Intensive Feelings Group each morning and found it challenging. In those sessions, patients sat on chairs arranged in a circle and discussed their present lives. They went around the circle, attempting to express how they felt. How lost. Confused. How turned upside down things had become. People regularly broke down and wept.

That first time, Liv ended up as a patient for several months. When he returned home, tired and withdrawn, nobody had a plan. Instead we approached each day hesitantly with a kind of imagined, invisible questionnaire clutched in our hands. It held all the questions we wanted to ask and couldn't.

How much will he want to talk about his disorder?

    (Not at all, as it turned out—not the disorder, nor about his plans.)

How much is too private or too intrusive to ask?

    (Silence greeted many questions. Was that discomfort? Anger? Or was the subject matter too tough, too hurtful, or too complicated to discuss?)

Can one expect the hallucinations to be gone forever?

    (I hoped so. I've got to say that of all the symptoms of schizophrenia, it was the hallucinations that disturbed me the most.)

How would he be to talk to?

    (Conversations were a hard go, initially.)

Could he return to his old job?

> (The answer to that one was no. His previous employers at the print shop were too alarmed, and though I had phoned ahead and held a meeting with the unit supervisor, the university inexplicably refused to recognize his disorder as an illness or give him medical leave. This only reinforced the impression that whatever Liv was suffering from, it was his fault.)

Would he be able to live independently or want to live independently?

> (That was anybody's guess. Nobody knew.)

Would he be able to sustain relationships outside the family?

> (The answer to that was complicated. In the end, the answer was yes, but the relationships were new ones that he had to develop over time.)

In the long run, would he be happy?

> (This was perhaps the most important question, and the one that was the most difficult to answer because it depended on a longer perspective. In the short-term, I'd have to say he was pretty unhappy.)

How complete would the recovery be?

> (That question is a big question—it is in fact *the* big question everyone has, and it isn't until later that you learn that it's the wrong question. Wrong because it isn't really a recovery. It is a new life, with a new and different way of relating to almost everything.)

Of course, Liv approached things with his own questionnaire, every bit as filled with uncertainties as ours.

Many of his questions were the same ones we asked but posed in reverse. For instance:

What do they want from me now that I'm back?
> (We didn't know. Couldn't have told him.)

Do they expect me to find a job?
> (I think the answer to that was probably yes. We hoped he would, eventually, lead an independent life.)

Will I be *able* to find a job?
> (We didn't know, but we certainly couldn't have anticipated how difficult it would be.)

Are they happy that I'm out of the hospital?
> (We were. Worried and anxious too but happy.)

Do they resent having me in the house again?
> (I don't think my parents did, but the routine around their home was changed pretty thoroughly.)

How are we all going to get along?
(Nobody knew.)

THIS MORNING I LISTENED
TO THE WIND BLOW AND
RAIN PATTER AGAINST MY
WINDOW

Though they couldn't be seen or actually touched, these two questionnaires were something we reviewed, filled out, and filed each day.

I DID NOT WANT TO
GET UP BUT MOM WAS
CALLING ME FOR
BREAKFAST

And the next day we started filling them out again from scratch.

I ATE BREAKFAST WITH MOM
I ASKED HER HOW SHE SLEPT
SHE SAID "FINE" BUT SHE
COULD HEAR THE WIND BLOW.

DAD MADE ME BACON AND EGGS WHEN
I GOT HOME IN THE MORNING

Liv was also diagnosed and treated for depression. He came by that honestly, since my father had an inclination toward pessimism that ran deep and in retrospect looked remarkably like depression.

Dad was a short, bald, rather formal man who regretted every decision he'd ever made. He had emigrated from the south of France to Canada following the war, and not a day passed that he didn't curse the colder climate and the flawed decision making that had led to the move. He spent his days preparing for the failures that he was sure were coming. He had lived hard through the Great Depression and consequently saved scraps of every useless kind—rubber bands, paper clips, old shoes of any size or disrepair, paper bags—preparing for the next economic downturn. (I was never sure how the paper bags were supposed to save us when bad times arrived. Would we corner the market on paper bags?) He trained us not to expect praise or celebrate anything immoderately. This kind of behaviour only tempted the fates, who were prone to savage you in an instant.

EUERY TIME HE LEFT
HOME HE WOULD SAY
DONT SET FIRE TO THE HOUSE

He was a fatalist. A numerologist. A dedicated believer in astrology. He plotted complicated astral charts and was convinced that you lived under either lucky or unlucky stars.

He didn't drive. He distrusted cars and almost all technological advances—and since his frame of reference tended to stop after the 1920s, technological advances included the video camera, the flush toilet, and the telephone. Most nights he spent seated on the rickety wooden chair in the corner of our tiny kitchen with the lights turned off. Alone in the dark, he rolled and then slowly smoked his thin, acrid cigarettes. If you passed him on the way to the washroom, he remained silent, but later, from the living room, you would hear him sigh heavily and then mutter, "Tout est perdu au Canada."

All Is Lost in Canada.
That seemed to pretty well cover everything.

MY DAD WAS AN UNHAPPY MAN. TOUT EST PERDU AU CANADA.

DAD AND I WENT
FOR WALKS

My father and mother struggled with their differences for years, but the death of my youngest brother eventually kicked over the foundations. The toxic combination of grief, guilt, shame, and blame chafed at them until it wore through the already-strained bonds of matrimony.

Thrifty and practical by nature, they settled matters out of court. My mother took possession of the house. My father was permitted to maintain his cramped office at home and come and go as he liked.

The divorce hit my father hard. He was, after all, in his seventies at the time and retired, so had no lofty ambitions for the future. He was also old-world enough to believe that his family, as turned inside out as we were, was his patrimony and his life's crowning achievement. The divorce threatened to put all that at risk. His solution was to secure a small apartment about a mile away from our home. He moved his meagre pile of belongings there and then committed himself to an unconventional daily regimen.

Each morning, he rose before sunrise and hiked back to our home. As my mother left to go to work, he would unlock and enter the home that was no longer his. He would take his former station, seated on the wooden chair in the kitchen.

There he would wait.

When Liv arose, they would first take a quiet breakfast together. Following that, my father would slip on his worn overcoat and his hat—in all his years, regardless of the weather, season, or informality of the occasion, I never saw my father go out anywhere without his overcoat and a broad-brimmed hat—and the two would set out on their daily walk. Together on foot, my dad and my restless brother crisscrossed the city.

When you lose a limb, I'm told, the whole body adjusts. The posture changes. You sit and stand differently.

The same thing happens to families when someone dies. Everyone shifts to compensate for the loss. Hiking with Liv was my father's compensation. He had held a conversation with himself and made a compact. This time he was intent on not losing sight of his son.

Even admitting the possibility of a relapse seems a kind of betrayal.

The implication is that you don't possess sufficient faith in the will of the individual to recover. It takes a while before you understand that it's not a matter of will. If it was only a matter of will, nobody would ever relapse (or develop the illness in the first place), and I don't know anybody who has received treatment for mental illness that hasn't experienced at least one serious relapse.

Liv experienced his first only a few months after he had been released.

He had been prescribed additional drugs to combat anxiety. These drugs, it turned out, had to be taken a particular way or else they responded badly with the other medication he was taking.

My oldest brother, Nic, has remained the most practical of the three remaining brothers, and the most reserved. He had always participated in the affairs of our family in his quiet and pragmatic ways. Thinking that Liv would appreciate a change of setting and a change of pace, Nic invited Liv along on his annual camping vacation.

The trip proved a disaster. It caught Liv at the moment that his inner chemistry, simmering for some time, boiled over. Each day of the vacation saw Liv grow increasingly agitated. Soon it became apparent that he was experiencing intense hallucinations. He became possessed by certain visions and refused to respond to questions. One evening, as the darkness settled at their campground, things came to a head. Liv fled the picnic table and slipped into a tangled cedar thicket.

Nic's wife was badly upset. Nic waded into the brush and worked hard to coax Liv back to the car, then hurriedly packed their tent and belongings. The drive home was harrowing. Harrowing for Liv because, it was clear, something was frightening him terribly; harrowing for Nic because he wasn't certain that Liv wouldn't leap from the car.

Nic didn't bother driving home. He drove directly to emergency services, waited with Liv while intake assessed him, and then watched as he returned to the psychiatric ward.

Part Four

This time, the stay in hospital was shorter.

His prescription modified, Liv was released and provided with the name of a community nurse he was to meet with on a regular basis. She would be his key resource and the person to help him make the transition from the hospital back into the community.

Which might have been fine, except that shortly after he checked out, the nurses union embarked upon a lengthy, bitter strike, and suddenly Liv had no medical support, nor any programs to attend. The city's psychiatrists were swamped, and Liv's medical liaison consisted of a single hour-long appointment held once a month.

I remember that period this way. For months after Liv returned, time weighed on him. He said nothing—maybe not nothing, but next to nothing.

He would sink into the couch and stare at the TV or gaze out the window. Occasionally he would murmur, "Oh well" dejectedly, which seemed in spirit to eerily echo my father's stock phrase "All is lost." His tongue, influenced by the drugs he had been prescribed, would restlessly dart in and out of his mouth. His legs would jiggle. Abruptly he would sigh loudly, launch himself from the couch, stand and stride out the door.

My father would call in his fractured English, "Where you go?" Liv would carry on without replying. Dad, throwing on his overcoat and hat as he crossed the front landing, would scurry after him.

I would at times drop by the house and sit vigil with Liv, hoping that he'd understand this attendance as an invitation to talk. That got us nowhere. Small talk of any kind was, I discovered, a pointless exercise. I tried asking him outright what he was feeling. That approach failed. Questions only made him impatient. Finally after weeks of this kind of tense, unproductive quiet, I resorted to my last and least likely strategy, a strategy that occurred to me only because I was at the time immersed in mailing out spec scripts to various theatres.

I drafted a letter.

In the letter I told Liv that we were scared. Scared because we didn't know what he was thinking or what need fuelled his walks. We didn't know where he was going. We didn't know what he expected to do, or what he expected of us. I explained that if he couldn't talk to me directly about how he was feeling, maybe he could write to me.

It was perhaps one indication of how thoroughly and obsessively steeped in writing culture I was at the time that I included a self-addressed, stamped envelope. I hurried to the post office and, fairly certain that my letter would be ignored, mailed it.

A week later I picked a letter out of my mailbox. It was my stamped, self-addressed envelope. A single wrinkled piece of foolscap was folded roughly in the envelope. Liv's spidery handwriting crawled across the page, but his prose was spare.

"Dear Clem," he wrote. "I don't hallucinate anymore, but now I don't feel much of anything. The drugs have flattened or erased every emotion I had. I don't know how to live like that, feeling nothing."

I picked up a pen and wrote. In my letter I asked him to wait. (And sometimes I think the entire body of my advice, over all the years we have talked and written, could be distilled into that one word. *Wait*. Wait—don't do anything hasty. Wait—things will get better. Wait until you receive more complete information. Wait until you've had a chance to consider things. Wait till this afternoon, wait till tomorrow.... Don't panic today, don't quit your job today. Wait.) I told him that in time he might begin to feel things again. I urged him to consider that it was still early in his treatment. I reminded him that although the nurses were on strike and he only saw his psychiatrist once a month, he could still use those visits to discuss these matters. His psychiatrist might dispense more effective advice than mine.

I folded the sheet. I slid it in another envelope, again inserted a self-addressed, stamped envelope, then drove to my parents' home and dropped it in the mailbox.

I received his letter a few days later.

We continued in this back-and-forth fashion for nearly a year. For whatever reasons, we couldn't find the correct words when we sat in a room together, but we could communicate with each other through the mail. With each letter I wrote, I included a self-addressed, stamped envelope.

Some of the letters I received from Liv were longer, others cryptically short. We kept writing. I remember being pleasantly surprised to feel that curious sensation of anticipation and excitement that accompanies waiting for something important to arrive in the mail.

Then, a little more than a year later, I was out of town for a theatre residence in another city and didn't come back to collect my mail for more than a week.

The night that I returned to Calgary I received a phone call. It was Liv asking me where his letter was.

From that point on—and for nearly twenty-five years—we spoke with each other on the phone every evening. Sometimes, if he was particularly worried about some matter, Liv would call several times—maybe three or four times within the space of three or four hours.

If he was in a positive mood, we might only spend fifteen or twenty minutes catching up on the day's events. If he was troubled, the conversation could last most of the night. I was never sure that I had the tools required to deal with the problems he broached—on several occasions I'm quite certain that I didn't—but if we spoke together long enough, and logged sufficient hours, he said he felt calmer.

Part Five

I have this game I like to play. You can play it too. I call it "Worst Jobs."

The game starts when you ask people at a party to describe the very worst job they've ever held. At first an awkward silence envelops the room as guests calculate what they feel comfortable sharing. Then comes the torrent as individuals respond, hesitant initially and then with greater candour and passion. The stories are sordid, strange, embarrassing, and nearly always generate the proper combination of disgust, horror, pathos, and pity, which are the truest ingredients of both comedy and tragedy.

Almost every job available to people with schizophrenia would make wonderful material for the "Worst Jobs" game.

A SPARROW GOT CAUGHT INSIDE
THE SECOND CUP

THE SPARROW WAS TERRIFIED!
IN THIS SAME WAY I WAS TRAPPED
I WAS TOLD BY AISH TO GO AS LONG
AS I COULD ON DISABILITY AND THE
INSURANCE

As the nurses continued their strike, Liv was initially left to his own devices. He walked to calm himself. Sometimes he spontaneously embarked upon long drives through the countryside. He also responded by job hunting.

It was a natural impulse. Pretty much the first thing people ask when they meet you is "What are you doing these days?" They say "doing," but that's just code. What they really want to know is what you're doing at *work*. If you can't answer that first and most principal question, you are left with a gaping void in your conversation— and in your identity.

I WAS WORKING AS A NIGHT WATCHMAN

My brother sought employment. His search was, of course, hampered by his inability to obtain references and by his obvious mental fragility. He looked troubled, and the side effects of his medication didn't help.

He kept after it, filling out applications, following up on a number of false leads until finally he hit a kind of perverse pay dirt. He was hired by a security firm as a night-duty guard.

Like many jobs of this kind, security work tends to recruit from those too old, undertrained, or marginalized to get jobs elsewhere. Liv's position apparently involved wearing an ill-fitting, pseudo-military-style blue-grey uniform (which he had to purchase), receiving the briefest, most primitive training (which, boiled down to its essence, was something like "be vigilant" and "never permit anyone to bite you"), and performing security rounds in a variety of difficult-to-reach, dangerous environments.

While he struggled with the side effects of the antipsychotic drugs, getting up each day despite crushing depression, trying—and mostly failing—to control his mounting paranoia, my brother slipped on his lopsided jacket, clipped on his tie, and punched in at ten each evening as the guard of a vast outdoor historical theme park.

At night the lights winked out in the log cabins, one-room schoolhouses, Old Tyme candy stores, smithies, barns, and storage sheds as the park was abandoned. Darkness quickly transformed the site into an eerie prairie ghost town. Strong winds swept off the reservoir and rattled bent cottonwoods. My brother crept through the brush at the perimeter of the park, flashlight in hand. On various occasions he stumbled upon drunks, vandals, would-be thieves, delinquents, couples messing around, discarded clothing, caches of drugs, and the occasional scared stray mule deer bursting from cover in an explosion of hooves and clattering antlers. Terrified that he might be confronted, Liv would often shout random warnings as he waded into the brush.

My family worried constantly about what might happen in the eventuality that an intruder didn't flee. The security company didn't provide guards with backup or so much as a nightstick or phone.

He would return home each morning tense, quickly consume a cold meal, and then collapse into bed. The next evening he'd rise, slip into his wrinkled uniform, and begin again.

WHEN I WAS A SECURITY
GUARD SOME ONE
TRIED TO BREAK INTO
C. J ROBERT JEWELRY

THE PEOPLE ACROSS
THE ALLEY SAW
THEM AND CALLED
THE POLICE

I MET SERGEANT KAY

HE TOLD ME THE
PHONE BOOTH WAS
AROUND THE CORNER

On a separate assignment as a security guard for a different firm, my brother was instructed to monitor a jewellery store that had been burglarized. The criminals had smashed a gaping hole in the rear brick wall.

Liv's duty was to guard that hole.

He waited at the site each night, stared into the shattered brickwork, and hoped that whoever had taken the time to orchestrate the break-in wouldn't return. He was provided with a long, heavy flashlight and a strip of paper with a phone number written on it. In the event that the criminals arrived, he was to outrun them to a pay phone down the block, where he was to call for help.

THERE IS NO FOOD ONLY
LIQUOR

FATSO YOU THINK
I CARE WHETHER
YOU HAVE BADGES!

WE WERE SUPPOSED TO GUARD
A PARTY. THE GUARD IN CHARGE
SAID THINGS WOULD BE OK.

THE BOSS GUARD TOLD ME TO
STAND IN THE FRONT OF THE
DANCE AREA. ONE GUY WANTED
TO FIGHT WITH ME.

The same security firm assigned him to maintain order and keep the peace at a local race track. Each night, the crowd would arrive laden with large plastic jugs heavy with booze. They watched cars and drank.

Once the races had concluded, the utterly toasted fans staggered cursing back to the parking lot. Liv's job was to prevent urination—an impossible task given the lack of sanitary stations—as well as drunken fights and vandalism.

I CALLED IN SICK BECAUSE I WAS AFRAID OF WOAK

I WAS A SECURITY
GUARD

I STARTED AT
GLENMORE PARK

PAUL WAS
THE GUY
WHO COVERED
THE OTHER
SHIFT

THE MOST STEALABLE HOSPITAL
STUFF IS THE TOOLS
IN THE MAINTENANCE DEPT.

His final security rounds were at a hospital. His
duties included patrolling the grounds, parking
lots, and wards. One evening Liv learned that his
gruff, no-nonsense partner, assigned to secure
another ward, was in fact routinely stealing
pharmaceuticals from the locked storage area.
When Liv returned from his rounds, he found
the police hustling his embarrassed colleague
into a squad car.

THE HEAD NURSE CAUGHT
PAUL AND ONE NURSE
STEALING TOOLS
ONE NIGHT

TEN -20 YEARS AGO
I WAS A SECURITY GUARD

I WAS ON STELAZINE
BUT WORKING AT
NIGHT WAS HARD

IT WAS HARD TO
CONFRONT PEOPLE

EVERY TWO WEEKS THERE
WAS PAY PARADE

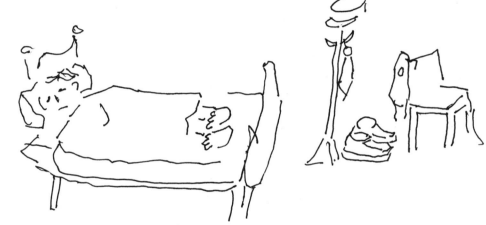

I WAS AFRAID TO GO TO PAY PARADE
MOST OF GUYS HAD BEEN IN THE SERVICE
I MISSED PAY PARADE A LOT OF THE TIME
DAD TOLD ME NOT TO DO THAT.

I REMEMBER WHEN I HAD A BETTER
JOB WORKING IN THE LABOUR CREW.
IF WE DIDN'T CROSS THE PICKETERS
WE WOULD WOULD BE FIRED
I WENT IN AT 6 SIX IN THE
MORNING WHEN THE PICKETERS
HAD JUST STARTED.   THE STRIKE
LASTED A DAY

The work had become a kind of trap. With each shift Liv grew more detached from every kind of meaningful human connection. Whatever assignment he accepted, he performed his rounds at night, which, in turn, began to increasingly inform his bleak outlook. The isolation gnawed at him. His paranoia grew. His mental situation deteriorated and delusions began to consume him. His community nurse and psychiatrist met, informed him that the security work was contributing to his illness, and urged him to quit.

MY MOM AND DAD SUPPORTED ME FOR A YEAR

Jobless again, Liv resumed his long walks with my father.

Liv had always been a cipher to my dad. My brother had displayed an artistic temperament from a very early age. When he graduated from high school, he had elected to enrol in art college. This inclination totally baffled my father.

Dad had trained in Marseille as an accountant. While he enjoyed opera, and would occasionally burst into a throaty aria, he didn't at all understand contemporary art. He was unable to see how Liv's studies could ever evolve into a genuine career and was frequently puzzled by the anarchic drawings, sculptures, and ceramic pieces that Liv executed and displayed. The clearest example of the yawning gulf that existed between my brother's aspirations and my father's perceptions arose during Liv's second year at art school—when my father proposed that Liv enlist in the army.

I WISH I HAD A GOOD CIGAR

Life is full of surprises, though. My brother's illness and unemployment combined with my father's divorce and retirement to create conditions that drew the two closer. As they stalked about Calgary together, they began, each in their own way, to *get* each other.

I recall the astonishment I felt when I entered the house one afternoon and observed my elderly father crouched on the floor on his hands and knees, demonstrating for Liv's benefit the downward dog and cat positions he'd learned at his seniors yoga classes.

On their rambles, they uncovered things that they had held in common. On the bitterest days of winter, the walks often concluded at the zoo, where my father could recover from the cold with a cup of hot chocolate, in the humid, glass-sided arboretum. There, they exchanged observations regarding philosophy, history, and my father's alternative, hybrid views on reli-gion—which involved something he occasionally and vaguely referred to as the "mystery of the dancing electrons."

DAD AND I WENT TO THE ZOO

MY BOY ALL YOU WANT IS TO GO TO THE ZOO

MY DAD AND I WENT AND HAD HOT DOGS AND COFFEE

DAD AND I WENT
FOR WALKS IN BOWNESS
PARK

DAD HAD SWOLLEN LEGS

HE BLACKED OUT AND
FELL ONCE GOING TO HIS APARTMENT

HE HAS POOR CIRCULATION
BUT I AM AN EMERGENCY
DOCTOR

One evening at the end of June, my father complained that he wasn't feeling 100 percent. He said he would take a light supper, and he returned to his apartment early. When he didn't come by for breakfast the next morning, Liv drove to his apartment.

No one answered the doorbell, so Liv found the maintenance man. They took turns knocking loudly at Dad's door, then the maintenance man inserted the master key into the lock and opened it. My brother entered the silent apartment and found my father's slight frame splayed across his bed.

It was a stroke, or a heart attack, or perhaps a stroke followed by a heart attack.

The funeral was short and difficult. Liv hung on for a few weeks, but it was quickly apparent that it couldn't last. A month and a half after my father died, Liv experienced another psychotic episode and a breakdown.

The first relapse is disheartening, the second an epiphany. You realize how unlike other medical conditions schizophrenia is.

A broken bone will mend. Even diseases regarded as serious can often be dispatched with the right mixture of clinical attention and drugs. Nothing can compel schizophrenia to pack up and leave for good.

At this point, you begin to understand. It can be monitored. To an extent it can be controlled. But that control is fragile, and it exists at the whim of so many things. If one delicate element falls out of balance, everything can crumble in an instant.

I TRIED TO WORK AT
A PRINTING PLANT

THE FOREMAN GARY
SAID I WAS STANDING
AROUND TOO MUCH
AND SAID HE WOULDN'T
BE CALLING ME ANYMORE

A little more than a month after Liv was released from hospital, he began searching for work outside the security industry. The inability to get anything gnawed at him. He followed up on ads and got no takers. Each failure confirmed his worst opinion of himself.

He tried returning to work with print companies, hoping that his former experience in the field would help. One company hired him, but the nervous twitching caused by the prescription drugs interfered with his running the machines. At the end of the first day, the boss reprimanded him in front of the other employees, said he was too slow, and fired him.

Liv returned home and collapsed on the couch. I was visiting at the time, and sat down next to him. What was there to say? It did no one any good to rehash the day's events. Every once in a while Liv would break the stillness to declare, "Oh well" and fall silent again.

"Oh well what?" I'd ask.

"Just, oh well."

I TOLD MY PSYCHIATRIST I WAS AFRAID TO PICK UP MY PAY CHEQUE. THE DOCTOR SAID IF I NEEDED THE MONEY SO BAD I WOULD BE THERE ON TIME.

Liv joined a job-finding club, received further counselling, took work as he could find it as a caretaker, a delivery person, a shipper-receiver, struggled daily to control his delusions and mounting paranoia until finally he was placed on disability. Looking back, I know our family had a positive influence on Liv. In his day-to-day-life we offered support when things spun out of control. I understand that. I also know that there were times that we didn't know what we were doing.

During those years when Liv searched for work and hated it, when he accepted crappy jobs that paid poorly, treated him like a serf, and made him crazy, we were sympathetic. But we still encouraged him to find and hold on to those jobs.

We were so programmed to believe that a life without work was a life without meaning.

Which pretty much put us in the same camp as nearly everyone else. For the longest time, even Liv's doctors urged him to hang in there, to hold on for dear life to whatever bone the job market might throw his way.

It's all based on fear, of course.

After all, what are you without a job? Invisible. A ghost. Less than a ghost: an unemployed ghost.

Interlude:
The Circles of Hell

To appreciate Liv's anxiety surrounding being unemployed, you have to understand that for those with mental illnesses, beneath the surface of society there exists another dimension, and it is always, always waiting.

It's a special dimension of Mental Health Hell, and it can best be evoked as a series of spiralling circles. The circles curl one into the other. Each represents an increasing torment.

Circle One

You wake up one day uncertain, sad, confused, and are diagnosed with a mental illness.

You have entered only the First Circle of Mental Health Hell.

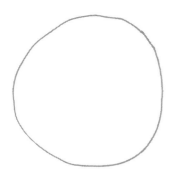

Circle Two

Oppressed by cares and concerns, unable to focus upon the necessities of life, you lose your job. Society places tremendous importance on employability and now, instead of a worthy citizen, you find you've morphed into a jobless, titleless nobody. You feel terrible—but worse things are in store.

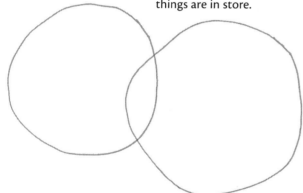

Circle Three

Your moods and behaviours alienate family
and friends, who now abandon you. Or, worse
luck, you didn't have family or friends around
to support you in the first place.

In any case, you find yourself on your own.
Truly on your own. With no one who understands
your frame of mind. No one to mediate on your
behalf. No backup. No adviser. No financial
support. And the Fourth Circle of Mental Health
Hell still attends.

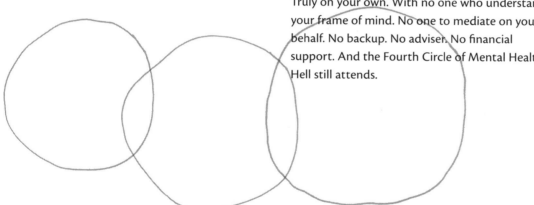

Circle Four

Your lack of income means that you can't continue to pay the rent or keep up with taxes, maintain car payments, afford groceries—or anything, really.

Unable to hold on to your home, you become homeless. You no longer have an illness. Instead, you find yourself transformed into an inconvenient, and largely ignorable, social condition.

Descend to the Fifth Circle of Mental Health Hell.

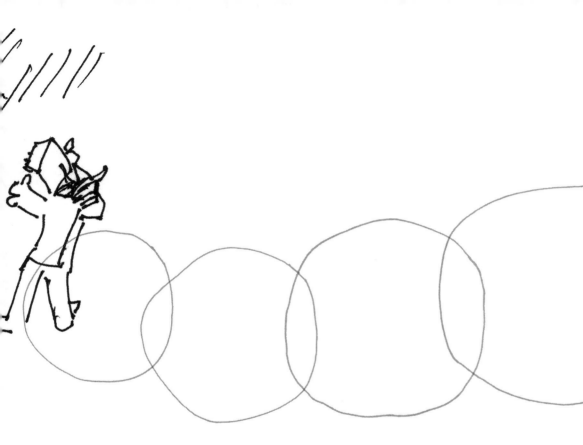

Circle Five

Fearful, uncertain of where to turn, untreated, you become feral. You roam the city, living in improvised stick shelters and hillside hollows. You do what you can to get the odd bit of money but are continually harassed by the authorities and intimidated and preyed upon by hooligans.

Because you are desperate to make a living, or because you are delusional and unable to clearly perceive the code under which everyone else operates, you transgress. You break the law in some way and the police arrest you. Incapable or unwilling to take advantage of legal assistance, you swiftly pass through an incomprehensible court system, are inducted into the final circle of Mental Health Hell, and go straight to jail, where you transform into the very worst kind of social condition, a prison statistic.

Abandon all hope as you settle in this most final destination, the Fifth Circle of Mental Health Hell.

SOON THE ~~THE~~ DRUG TRADE WILL BE LEGAL THERE WILL BE CRANK AND CRACK EVERYWHERE EVEN IN QUAKER OATS.

THE CITY IS TALKING ABOUT A RED LIGHT DISTRICT FOR SEX ADDICTS.

THE ONLY PLACE I FIT IN IN THIS SOCIETY IS BEGGING.

WOULDN'T IT BE EASIER
TO BE BURNED AT THE
STAKE

146

Part Six

These fears of marginalization may seem exaggerated, but for some, unfortunately, they are anything but. Liv has been extremely anxious at different stages in his life, consumed with fear that he might fall off the edge and become homeless, but then again he's travelled in circles where being homeless is a genuine career option. A number of his peers have ended up on the streets.

Part of his particular experience can be understood as a result of when he was first diagnosed—at the height of the Great Closing of the Eighties.

RALPH KLEIN BLEW UP
THE GENERAL HOSPITAL

The Great Closing was a time when governments concluded that the large psychiatric institutions were counterproductive. These impersonal, ineffective, very expensive institutions would be terminated, so the theory went, so that smaller, more effective programs could be implemented to integrate patients with mental illness into local communities. The resulting savings would generate the necessary funds to finance workshops and clinics, hire therapists and health care workers—all who would be essential to the effective facilitation of any successful integration.

THE HEALTH MINISTER SAID MENTAL ILLNESS IS AN EXCUSE FOR BAD BEHAVIOUR

Then along came the unanticipated recession of the Eighties.

Budgets eroded and all those lovely plans for integration and facilitation evaporated. The institutions closed all right, but—government health funding priorities being what they are—the essential financing that was supposed to follow people with mental illness into the communities never did.

NIETZSCHE ~~HEGEL~~ SAID THERE WILL NEVER BE
JUSTICE AS LONG AS PEOPLE HAD DIFFERENT
LEVELS OF POWER THE STRONG WILL
PREY ON tHE WEAK

Instead, we entered the beginning of an epoch that I refer to as Laissez-faire Health Care. *Laissez-faire* means "let be" or "leave alone," and never has anyone invented a more appropriate term when it comes to how governments have elected to treat mental health issues.

In Laissez-faire Health Care, there's a striking difference between how psychiatric patients and patients with all other ailments are treated, and the difference isn't a good one. Psychiatric patients are certainly "let alone." In fact, I'd suggest that this present "letting alone" by our health care system has conspired to beggar psychiatric patients—and I mean that quite literally.

Go out on the streets and look about. How many of those begging for a living have a mental illness? According to the U.S. Department of Health and Human Services Substance Abuse and Mental Health Services Administration, one of the biggest predictors for homelessness is untreated mental illness. The Treatment Advocacy Centre states that one-third of the homeless have an untreated mental illness. The blog Anxiety, Panic & Health puts it higher, at 45 to 50 percent, and the Canadian federal government's report *Mental Illness, Homelessness and the Criminal Justice System in Canada* maintains that 66 percent of homeless persons have a lifetime diagnosis of mental illness.

The appearance of people with mental illness on our streets in the numbers you see today coincides almost directly with the Great Closing of the Eighties.

Olivier was diagnosed in the very middle of that Great Closing. Since that time, he has been an outpatient with at least two psychiatric units that have seen their doors shut and their budgets vaporized. One unit had only just been renovated. The hospital, brand-new renovations and all, was abandoned.

Another unit was blown to kingdom come when Calgary's General Hospital was dynamited. It was a spectacularly symbolic demonstration of the new order. Programs that were offered when Liv was first diagnosed—group therapy sessions, occupational therapy, recreational therapy—shrivelled, shrank, and disappeared, never to be seen again.

EMERGENCY AMBULANCE ENTRANCE

EMS

The current approach insists that people with mental illness will do better integrated into the community rather than segregated and institutionalized. Which would make perfect sense except for two serious impediments: the government won't fund it and society won't tolerate it.

Ours is a culture indisposed to express anything beyond a fearful, barely concealed loathing when it comes to those manifesting mental illness. It won't make room for those who are ailing from it and does everything possible to exclude them.

Don't believe it? Let me invite you on two treasure hunts.

For Treasure Hunt Number One, travel to your local hospital. Doesn't matter which. Any will do. Walk through the front doors and observe what the hospital is proudest of. This shouldn't be hard to determine. It's generally where central administration has devoted the greatest amount of money—and symbols of that commendation will be everywhere.

Somewhere close by, prominently displayed, will be a large sign pronouncing the unit for Heart Disease and Strokes. Nearby you'll find a banner announcing the Neonatal Clinic. Perhaps you will read directions from a colourful poster guiding you to the Women's Health Centre or the Cancer Unit.

Now find the psychiatric ward.

Don't be worried if it takes a little time. It'll turn up eventually, secreted in some anonymous, out-of-the-way site.

Underfunding of psychiatric services is prevalent, systemic, and blithely accepted across the country. Only recently our regional health system in Calgary was required to find budget cuts for a new hospital that was being built. The first item eliminated was the psychiatric wing. Never mind that there was already an acknowledged, desperate city-wide shortage of bed space for psychiatric patients. The brand-new children's hospital was comparatively well funded but unfortunately experienced cuts in one area as well. Where?—the psychiatric unit. In 2002, the federal government described mental health as the "orphan child" of health care; myriad government reports tabled since then indicate that not much has changed.

Of course, champions of Laissez-faire Health Care maintain that hospital beds aren't essential because psychiatric care has been decentralized. Psychiatric patients don't *require* accommodation in hospitals anymore precisely because they have been so fully integrated into the community. Which brings us to Treasure Hunt Number Two. Find the integrated mental health support services.

Again, it may take you a while. If you'd like, you can consult your local directory and city map, feel free—but here's a hint. Don't bother looking in the Rosedales or Mount Royals or any other similarly affluent district.

Scout out your community's sketchiest, most criminalized districts. When you come upon the local needle exchange and halfway houses, you'll know you're getting hot.

To which health authorities respond that these are the areas where those with mental health issues live. Shouldn't their programs be located nearby?

True—and a bit of the chicken and egg. A significant percentage of people with mental illness can't hold down jobs. Governments insert a grudging hand into their change purses and dole out the most miserly stipend for living assistance for those they determine have severe handicaps. (The Alberta government provides $1,188 a month, as of this writing.) It follows that the only districts that people with mental illness can possibly afford to live in are in the most underdeveloped areas of town. Governments then capitalize on the situation by planting their few struggling social programs in a city's decaying strip malls—where they will obtain the least expensive leases.

Ensuring once again that if the mental health system can't *actually* provide adequate health care, it will certainly be the most cost-effective program the federal and provincial governments have ever operated.

To make matters worse, people with mental illness, with their particular habits and obsessive social behaviours, often present as visible targets. The criminal element, situated in close proximity, knows to the day when those on government assistance receive their cheques. People with mental illness are often harassed by a host of unsavory characters who queue up to panhandle, extort cash, and beg for cigarettes.

Running the gauntlet to the programs can prove so intimidating that individuals who could benefit most from therapy often abandon their quest and stay home.

Ultimately, however, the success or failure of any program should have some kind of statistically verifiable proof. And there, at least, things could not be clearer. Over the past decade, the gap in lifespans between those with mental health problems and those without has actually widened by more than ten years.

That's not a hidden secret. That's public knowledge. As early as 2007, an obscure little journal called *USA Today* reported that: "Adults with serious mental illness treated in public systems die about 25 years earlier than Americans overall, a gap that's widened since the early '90s when major mental disorders cut life spans by 10 to 15 years...."

More recently, another obscure periodical, *TIME* magazine, reported that data from sixteen states suggested that on average: "People with severe mental illness die 25 years earlier than the general population."

Canada's situation in this regard almost exactly parallels the United States'. In statistics released by the Conference Board of Canada in 2008, Canada and the United States were ranked side by side, in sixth and seventh positions out of sixteen nations, for rates of mortality due to mental illness.

Twenty-five years represents an enormous disparity. It represents more than a quarter of the average lifespan. If this statistic surfaced in reference to any other health condition, the fact that the gap has ballooned to the extent that it has would provoke outrage. A health crisis would be declared. People would be wearing ribbons and marching. Not so with mental illnesses.

The notion of integrating people with mental illness into the community is well intentioned, but it ignores the fact that without a central coordinating mechanism, it can be nearly impossible to monitor health care needs consistently.

Over the course of his illness, my brother has been assigned five different psychiatrists, a score of therapists, and I don't know how many community nurses. It's astonishingly easy for people with mental illness to fall through the cracks. Social programs are funded and then axed, the therapists transfer regularly, and nobody but nobody is positioned to track serious health problems when they arise.

The other seriously overlooked issue is that people with mental illness simply don't receive the same standard of health care as others do. Again, this isn't a secret, nor is it just my opinion. A recent study indicated that following a heart attack, people with mental illness were less likely than the general public to receive state-of-the-art treatment. Or to put it more bluntly, Wendy Brennan, executive director of the National Alliance on Mental Illness, characterized things this way: "Medical doctors think, 'Well, they're crazy,' so they don't take their concerns seriously."

In exchange for institutionalization, people with mental illness today have been provided with splendid autonomy. But this particular brand of autonomy comes with a price. It's an autonomy that allows them to survive however they may: on their own if they can, in the homes of their families if they require support—if they happen to have families available to support them—or on the streets and in prisons if they don't.

In any case, the beauty of this system is that the treatment they presently receive is killing them earlier than ever, so there will be less cost to the system than ever.

I HAD STATUS ALBEIT A VERY LOW STATUS

MY WORST FEAR IS I WILL END UP DUMPSTER DIVING

So, if Liv felt anxiety about not working, and consequently being unable to provide for himself or maintain financial control of his destiny, and if my family was also nervous about his not working, and all of us worried together that there might not be any mechanism to support him—we were probably right to worry.

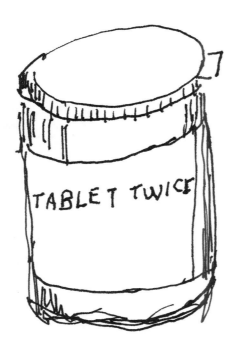

Part Seven

When I was younger, I thought that I had mapped out the lives of my family with certainty, but I've discovered that a life can be charted in many ways.

The medication in Liv's life has played such a key role in treatment—positively and negatively—that it's almost possible to plot the coordinates of my brother's existence based solely on the drugs he's been prescribed.

Liv's health, mobility, acuity, energy, and temperament have all been heavily influenced by the type and amount of pharmaceuticals he's taken. Over the years, his medication has been a constant, delivered in all shapes and sizes. It's been administered as injections, positioned like party treats in Dixie cups, and delivered as handfuls of cheery multicoloured pills to be swallowed.

THERE WAS A WOMAN IN
ROMANIA TRANSYLVANIA TO
BE EXACT WHO CONVINCED
SOME NUNS SHE WAS POSSESSED

SO SHE WAS CHAINED
TO A CROSS BY A PRIEST

THE PRIEST GAVE THE
BOOT TO THE DEVIL

Way back in dim pharmaceutical prehistory when the psychiatric establishment first abandoned cold-water baths, lobotomies, electroshock, and other bizarre forms of clinical witchcraft as principal therapies for schizophrenia, a handful of antipsychotic medications emerged on the landscape as the drugs of choice.

When the antipsychotics were first introduced, they were considered miracle drugs. They could be mass-produced relatively cheaply and could be counted on to permit those with schizophrenia to lead relatively independent lives.

Stelazine (trifluoperazine) was the particular drug administered to Liv early in his treatment, nearly thirty years ago. (It was also the drug prescribed to Ben.) Taken regularly, it eliminated most of his hallucinations. It also diminished his paranoia and had a positive influence on his mood disorders. On the other hand, it had a long and nasty history of undesirable side effects. The tension generated in this duality—benefit versus harm—has affected the treatment of mental illness since the very beginning of pharmaceutical treatment.

People often don't understand the ambivalent relationship that mental health patients have with their drugs. The general public wonders why so many psychiatric patients interrupt, abandon, or resist their medication. But it's legitimate to feel anxiety about taking a medication that, on the one hand, may dispel the voices you hear and permit you to interact with society but, on the other, may end up crippling or killing you.

I WENT TO WEDNESDAY EVENING GROUP

HE SAID TO ME "I WISH I COULD GIVE YOU SOMETHING ELSE BUT THERE ISN'T ANYTHING"

I'll STAY ON STELAZINE SO I CAN KEEP MY JOB

ONE OF THE PSYCHIATRISTS WAS IN CHARGE OF THE GROUP

My brother took Stelazine for more than a decade and a half, but within the first few months of treatment, serious side effects appeared. He developed all the signs of tardive dyskinesia— a disorder that manifests itself in involuntary, repetitive movements. In Liv's case, it also included restless tongue, rigidity, and tremors.

His hands shook and his fingers twitched as though he were stroking something. His legs trembled. He developed a frozen expression and would rock in place when he stood still. He grew unable to lift heavy objects or manipulate delicate ones.

He also developed something called akathisia, a condition described as a painful inner feeling or anxiety driving an individual to move. Although a person stands perfectly still, it is as though, inside, a motor is always running.

The entire time that Liv was on Stelazine, he paced restlessly and swayed.

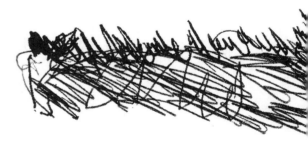

The explicit tradeoff has always been that the drugs permitted my brother to remain lucid. And the irony has been that while he is more aware and more in control of his thoughts—more truly himself—while continuing to take his medication, the drugs have had the effect of making him appear more agitated, more disturbed, and more dysfunctional to the rest of the world.

What makes taking the drugs particularly problematic is that over time, the side effects can be cumulative.

In the 1990s, it became apparent that Liv's physical condition was deteriorating. It had become difficult for him to perform even day-to-day tasks: to write, to fasten buttons, to secure zippers.

Tardive dyskinesia in most respects resembles Parkinson's syndrome. After a certain point there's a risk that it will become a permanent condition, with all the hazards associated with Parkinson's, regardless of whether the medication is discontinued.

I remember watching Liv's hands tremble as he held a drink I'd poured him one afternoon, wondering whether the glass would slip from his grasp. On another occasion, he tumbled from a stool as he tried to fix a lamp.

Eventually, things came to a head. Liv's doctors, nurses, and his attending psychiatrist consulted and decided that Liv had passed a threshold. His situation was no longer tenable; it was important that he stop taking Stelazine.

The question that followed, though, was, which new treatment would replace it?

Generally, when a psychiatrist speaks of a "new treatment," it means an alternative medication. This time Largactil was selected.

Largactil, or Thorazine, or chlorpromazine —the drugs always go by many brand and generic names—was another of the antipsychotic medications. One of the problems with the antipsychotics is that, because they all pretty much operate in the same way—blocking the receptors to the dopamine pathways in the brain—to a certain degree they all manifest a similar spectrum of side effects.

In Liv's case, after a time it became apparent that Largactil didn't diminish the tardive dyskinesia. It did, however, have its own disconcerting side effects.

Largactil can generate high levels of milk-producing hormones in the blood. As a result, soon Liv was not only dealing with the familiar and serious menu of nervous tics and twitches, but with hyperprolactinemia—he was beginning to develop swollen breasts and express milk.

Eight months after Liv had begun taking Largactil, the prescription was discontinued.

At this point, Liv's psychiatrist recommended that he switch to one of the new generation of antipsychotic drugs, Risperdal (risperidone).

Risperdal prescribed in conjunction with Luvox (fluvoxamine), an antidepressant, proved to be more effective in diminishing my brother's paranoid thoughts and anxieties but represented only marginal improvement in halting his shaking, twitching, and rocking.

Although different combined dosages of Risperdal and Luvox were explored over several years, eventually the pairing was found wanting, and it became necessary to move to another entry on the pharmaceutical list.

This resulted in a prescription of Olanzapine (a.k.a. Zalasta, Zolafren, or Olzapin).

For a time it seemed effective. The tremors and rocking slowly dissipated. We—my family and I—all breathed a little easier.

Olanzapine wasn't very helpful in regards to his paranoia, however. I remember speaking with Liv one evening, a few months after he'd commenced taking the new medication. He was upset about whether some people in the waiting room of a clinic had been talking about him.

This had been a common feature of Liv's paranoia —fears that he sometimes referred to as "dark whisperings." Essentially it was the notion that someone—sometimes acquaintances, sometimes total strangers—were plotting to do something to him.

SO I KNEW PEOPLE DID NOT LIKE ME ON THE SECOND FLOOR.

ON THE SECOND FLOOR I HEARD AN EVIL WHISPER

(If you have a mental illness, however, there's a better than average chance that someone *is*, in fact, talking about you. It's astonishing, actually. People do it all the time on public transportation. It's as though they believe that people with mental illness have experienced hearing loss as well.)

I COULDN'T FIND WHO SAID THE WORDS

As Liv and I chatted over the phone, I argued—as I always argued—that it was unlikely that people were actually *plotting* against him. Liv would see people talking and just assume that they were talking about him. My point was that the individuals in question could have been talking about anything at all.

Maybe, I told Liv, they were discussing the weather, maybe they were critiquing last night's television program. There was a distant possibility that they might have mentioned him, yes—but even then the context could be completely innocent and unimportant. Maybe they were talking about the colour of his shirt, or wondering whether they recognized him from somewhere. And in any case, even if there was some idle, irresponsible conversation about him, that didn't mean that anyone was plotting.

Liv wasn't buying it and remained unconvinced. "You don't understand," he told me.

"What don't I understand?" I asked.

"Everything."

We arrived at a compromise. If, at the end of the week, he still felt sufficiently upset, he would take the matter up with his nurse at his next appointment. This arrangement was one we often arrived at. Generally, by the end of a week, Liv would have concluded that his concerns were more a matter of his "ruminations" than somebody actually persecuting him.

But as we finished our phone call, I heard something in his voice that caught my attention. I asked him about it, and he told me he thought he might be coming down with a cold. I urged him to get some sleep, and to stop fretting so much about what people were saying.

I WAIT IN THE RAIN FOR A BUS.

But the next evening when he called again, he didn't sound any better. His voice was hoarse in a way that was different from your standard cold-in-the-throat rasp. And he was slurring his words. He complained that he'd slept fitfully.

I asked whether it was the flu. He replied that he didn't know what it was, but that it was making him dead tired. He told me that he'd been on his way to his art class at Self-Help after his Peer Options Group but had instead turned around and come home.

He added, as an afterthought, that while he was waiting for the bus he had almost blacked out. That caught me off guard.

"You mean, like, *fainted*?" I confirmed.

"Yes," he said.

"You better get to emergency," I urged him. "Fainting can be serious."

"No, no," he insisted. "I didn't actually fall down."

"Did you, or didn't you?"

There was a pause.

"Nearly."

There's an annoying trait my family has.

It emerges whenever there's any physical illness. It manifests itself in a kind of perverse, stoic pride in enduring a sickness regardless of the degree of discomfort or severity. Nothing—you will be informed—is ever as bad as it seems.

No discomfort is ever sufficient to warrant seeking assistance. You don't take pain medication. You don't trouble doctors. You avoid visiting hospitals unless you've stopped breathing or some internal organ has dropped out.

My father, in all his years as an accountant, never missed a day of work as a result of illness. For years I would miserably attend classes at school despite high fevers or racking coughs, until one day I realized that the rest of the world just called in sick and stayed home.

Liv displayed this family trait when he explained to me that he already had an appointment booked to see the doctor at the end of the week. He would, he told me, take the matter up of "nearly" fainting with the doctor then, if it was still bothering him.

I argued that the end of the week was a long way off, but Liv can be very stubborn. He just grows increasingly quiet until you realize ten minutes later that you've been talking to yourself.

Later that night, he called again, and this time there was no doubt that something was up. His voice was raspy and oddly high-pitched, nearly unrecognizable. He wheezed that he felt hot. He told me he was having trouble walking.

"Call an ambulance," I insisted.

In the background I could hear my mother agreeing with me, but Liv wouldn't do it. It would be expensive, he explained, and the condition would probably turn out to be nothing. Or perhaps the ambulance would take him to emergency, where the health authorities would scoff at his feeble inability to cope and send him home.

CLEM DROVE ME TO
THE ROCKY VIEW.

I couldn't make any sense of his logic, and in any case my aggravation with the situation was more than I could take. I told him I was on my way over.

Liv and Mom had recently moved into a condominium only a few minutes from where I lived. When I arrived at their place and saw him, I was shocked. He looked terrible—slumped in a chair, sucking in air and soaked in sweat.

We made our way out the front door and I loaded him into the car.

The drive from the condominium to the hospital normally takes forty-five minutes. I switched on the high beams and put my foot on the gas.

It was spring and cold, but he'd rolled the window all the way down. Wind swept through the car and his collar flapped. He craned his head out like a panting dog and still he sweated.

I couldn't figure out how things had gone so wrong so quickly. I kept him talking, though by this time I couldn't really be certain of what he was saying.

Then all at once he stopped answering me. I glanced over just as his head dropped and lolled onto one shoulder.

My medical training is limited to what I pick up from TV. I tend to assume that anything that involves gasping for air, sweating, and passing out is a heart attack. That's what I figured this was, with a stroke presenting an outside possibility.

My brother is dying, I thought, and we're still nearly fifteen minutes from anybody who can do anything about it.

I sped up, kept driving with one hand, and with the other performed the only medical procedure that came to mind. I poked him. He didn't respond, so I slapped his shoulder and shouted. This time he lifted his sweaty head and opened his eyes.

THE SECURITY GUARD TOLD ME
TO LINE UP AT ADMITTING

We pulled into the emergency bay of the hospital. I cut the motor, hopped out, and helped Liv from the car. Once inside, we were directed to line up at emergency intake. After a few minutes, an admittance person saw Liv and asked him to describe his problem.

I was so completely freaked by what had happened that I couldn't understand why Liv wasn't being attended to quicker, why someone hadn't jumped up to help us. Then I realized, as the intake nurse impatiently took the information from Liv, that with his staggering, slurring, and incomprehensible speech he must appear drunk.

I tried to intervene but was rebuked. She wanted to speak with him, not me. So she continued peppering him with questions that he answered only poorly in his squeaking, raspy voice, which she in turn misunderstood. Finally he provided her with his hospital identification number.

Instead of speeding things up, the process slowed even further. She directed us to sit and wait. Eventually, she said, we would be called.

EMERGENCY

NEXT

THE NURSE WAS RIGHT
IF I HAD ANY BRAINS I WOULD HAVE CHECKED
IN WITH ADMITTING IN THE FOOT HILLS.
I WAS NOT IN ANY PAIN I WAS JUST TIRED

I sat down hard beside Liv, stunned. I had broken speed limits to get to the hospital only to have him take his seat in the emergency room where, apparently, he would be permitted to expire.

But then it occurred to me that the nurse, having accessed Liv's previous hospital records and determining that he had been registered as a psychiatric patient, simply assumed Liv was experiencing a psychotic episode. And psychotic behaviour, on its own, won't kill you. Psychotic behaviour, in and of itself, doesn't constitute an emergency.

I returned to the intake nurse and we argued. I insisted that this was *not* Liv's normal behaviour, nor was it a psychotic episode. This was different. I told her that Liv had complained of blacking out earlier in the day and had suddenly passed out in the car ride to the hospital.

Something I said seemed to make a difference because she took some notes and left. Minutes later she reappeared and asked Liv to follow her to another station, where a blood sample was taken.

A short time lapsed before she returned, and this time real health care kicked in. The difference was striking. Everything was organized. Everything was guided by purpose. Everything moved quickly. The intake nurse was accompanied by an attendant, who helped Liv into a wheelchair.

He was whisked through the big double doors. They flapped shut behind him as he disappeared.

It turns out it wasn't a heart attack or a stroke. It was diabetes.

I was completely blindsided by this because Liv hadn't ever been diagnosed as diabetic. How had this disorder been missed, given that Liv attended regular appointments with his doctor? How had it appeared so quickly, and with such severity?

I learned later that his doctor told him that in his thirty years of medical practice, he'd never seen blood sugar levels like the ones Liv had that night.

I GET THIS GUY A WHEEL CHAIR

Six years after Liv was prescribed olanzapine and experienced his diabetic attack, I came across an online *New York Times* article that indicated that there hadn't been full disclosure about the potentially dangerous impact of the medication Zyprexa. (Zyprexa is one of the many brand names that olanzapine is sold under.)

The article presented testimony that had emerged during a court case indicating that the risks of a diabetic attack had been well known to the pharmaceutical company.

"... [T]he documents introduced in Courtroom 403 show that for much of the last decade, Lilly executives played down those risks. Among themselves, in internal e-mail messages and memorandums, they shared worries that Zyprexa's sales would fall if the drug was linked to weight gain or diabetes."

A little stunned, I clicked on a hypertext link at the bottom of the page. Another article popped up, describing a class-action suit launched against Eli Lilly. More than eighteen thousand claimants. Further allegations of suppressed information. Individuals who abruptly developed diabetes and hyperglycemia. Individuals who had died.

When I finished reading, I had to sit quietly for a long, long moment. I cannot fully describe how betrayed I felt.

As far as Liv had known, as far as we all—everyone in our family—had known, from everything we had been told, and from all the information we had received at the hospitals and from the medical practice, Liv's sudden diabetic reaction had simply been an unfortunate, unexpected, unusual response to his medication. Nothing immediately after, or in the six years following, had led us to believe otherwise. No information had been provided to suggest that anyone could have done anything to prevent it.

Then along came this article, calling everything into question.

I thought back to Liv's diabetic attack. How swift its onset had been, and severe. The long-term impact diabetes has had upon his life. To learn that people in a position of influence had known of the risks associated with this drug, and then to understand that they had *chosen* not to promote the facts. To understand that what happened to my brother had meant that little to them.

I called Liv and we discussed the article. After looking more closely into the events, and following our communication with a legal firm, Liv elected to join one of the several class-action suits that have resulted from the release of this previously hidden information. That action is currently before the courts.

Part Eight

Because the olanzapine generated such a severe diabetic spike, my brother was forced to switch medications once again.

This time the particular drug selected was Seroquel (a.k.a. Ketipinor, or quetiapine).

I TAKE MY METFORMIN AND LIPITOR AT BREAKFAST

I USED TO TAKE HUMULIN WITH A SYRINGE

THE DOCTOR TOLD ME MY SUGARS ARE 9.9 AVERAGE

As a result of the diabetes, Liv now had a whole other level of medical routines to deal with. There were needles he had to administer, blood levels that had to be monitored. It was important that he pay closer attention to his diet.

I could see that these additional procedures had an impact on him, that he felt that his life was becoming increasingly complicated and defined by his multiple medical conditions.

It changed his mood. At first I thought he simply felt anxious because of all the new procedures. After all, if I had suddenly developed diabetes, I might have been upset. Then I glanced up at him one afternoon and noticed a distant expression on his face, as though he was listening to something.

A NURSE ASKED ME IF I WOULD HARM MYSELF OR MY MOTHER. I WAS AFRAID TO ANSWER BECAUSE I WAS AFRAID WHAT IT WOULD SAY ON MY PERMANENT RECORD.

AFTER A LONG TIME I SAID NO.

A month later, I began to detect signs that Seroquel wasn't going to do the trick. Liv had begun to quietly talk to himself again. When he came over to visit with the family, I'd find him sitting in a room off by himself, staring out the window.

"What's out the window?" I'd ask.

"Nothing," he'd answer but continue to look.

Liv and I are close. There are times when we've had to talk a number of difficult things through. That doesn't mean that he shares everything with me. He's a private individual and there are things that he keeps to himself.

Whatever he was feeling at that time suddenly reached a point of crisis. His psychiatrist, concerned for his safety, abruptly signed an admittance order for the hospital.

I received a phone call from Liv. He said his psychiatrist had told him not to go home but instead go directly to the hospital and check in through emergency.

I said I'd drive him to the hospital and accompany him in.

SO I WENT INTO HOSPITAL

I WAS PUT IN A ROOM WHERE I JUST SAT.

The problem with getting admitted through emergency is that, unlike the personnel who staff psych wards and regularly deal with individuals with mental health issues, the folks who operate emergency units don't have any special understanding of, or appreciation for, this clientele. Trained to deal with problems in the escalating order of their urgency, emergency unit staff perceive people with mental illness—with their long, rambling stories, their imprecise diagnoses—as a nuisance to the smooth running of their necessary operations.

You see those signs in emergency waiting rooms that say you will be taken care of in the order of the severity of your illness? Those signs guarantee that if you have arrived at the emergency room with a mental health crisis, unless you are clutching a can of lighter fluid in one hand and are threatening self-immolation, you will be the very last person to be looked after.

When we arrived at emergency, we were told the psychiatric unit was full, but if Olivier would just take a seat, they would find him a bed.

I sat with Liv for several hours. Eventually I received assurances that admittance would happen later that night and he would be taken care of. I told him I'd come back the next day to see how he was settling in. Liv left a message on my machine later that evening to say that he was being moved.

I WENT INTO THE ROOM.

I WAS GIVEN SOME PYJAMAS TO WEAR

I GOT A MEAL WHICH I ATE

I FELL ASLEEP ON A COT
IN THE ROOM

I REMEMBER WAKING
UP AND SEEING A FACE
FLOATING ABOVE ME BUT
I DON'T REMEMBER WHAT
SHE SAID.

THE NEXT MORNING I WAS
ON A GURNEY IN THE
HALL WAY.

I TRIED TO HOLD
CONVERSATIONS WITH
PEOPLE WHO WERE
ALSO IN THE HALL WAY

The next morning I returned to the hospital. He was no longer in the lobby, but when I inquired at admissions, I was told that he hadn't yet received a room. After some investigation, I found him alone and still waiting. He had been moved—but the movement had only extended as far as a dark, secluded side alcove in the emergency unit, where he had been provided with a sheeted gurney, a pillow, and a meal on a tray.

He had been parked there most of the evening.

I walked down the hallway and asked the receiving attendant when she anticipated that a bed on the unit would be ready. I was assured that it would be "soon."

I went to work worried. When I returned later that afternoon, they still hadn't found a bed on the unit.

When I left that night, Nic stopped by the hospital and visited. The next day I returned and inquired whether a room had been found yet, but was told that the situation remained the same. When I went looking for Liv, though, I found the spot where he'd last been sitting deserted. Only the gurney, the empty food tray, and a glass of water suggested that he'd ever been there. Perhaps he'd gone to the washroom. I sat down. Minutes passed.

I stood again and began searching for him in the hallways and other cubicles. Half an hour later, nothing.

I returned to admissions. Did anyone have any idea where he might be? I asked. Though he had been signed into the care of the hospital, nobody on the emergency team could tell me his precise location. One distracted nurse felt certain he had left a short while ago to get something to eat. Another said he was certain Olivier had checked out and gone home, but that wasn't indicated anywhere by his signature.

It became pretty clear that nobody knew for sure.

If you've experienced a suicide in your family, it is the very first place your mind turns when someone goes missing. I knew Liv was in trouble. I knew his psychiatrist felt the situation was serious.

I returned to the hallways and again found no sign of him, and at that point began to panic. I scanned the lobby. Nothing. I checked the elevators. I went out to the parking lot. Nothing.

I ANSWERED THE VOICE.

I THEN NOTICED A NURSE SHE ASKED IF I WANTED A BLANKET. I SAID "NO, I WOULD RATHER STAY COLD"

I NOTICED THE NURSE HAD TEARS IN HER EYES.

LATER A MAN LED ME
TO ANOTHER ROOM.

THE ROOM HAD MANY
CURTAINS AND I HAD
A BED

I STAYED AWAKE
ALL NIGHT AT LEAST
I THINK I DID BECAUSE
I WATCHED THE CLOCK.

WHEN MORNING CAME THE ROOM HAD THREE SECURITY GUARDS AT THE DOOR.

CAN I GO OUT?

I ASKED THE GUARD AT THE DOOR IF I COULD LEAVE. HE SAID "SURE!" AS IF HE WASN'T THERE FOR ME.

I SAW TWO MEN TALKING ONE LOOKED LIKE ANDY FROM WORK. BUT I WAS AFRAID TO TALK TO HIM.

— CAN I GO OUT SIDE

At last I found him wandering the hospital grounds. He had hallucinated throughout the night and most of the day. Disoriented by the isolation, beginning to fear that the hospital staff were organizing some kind of action against him, he had split. No one questioned him. No one tried to stop him.

We sat on a bench and I encouraged him to return to emergency. He wasn't convinced that it was a good idea but finally agreed.

I WENT OUTSIDE

A CAR DROVE BY A MAN YELLED OUT OF THE CAR AT ME.

I PHONED MY MOTHER BECAUSE I HEARD SHE HAD AN ACCIDENT AND HAD DIED.

After he had settled back in his alcove, I asked a nurse whether she thought it was wise to place someone paranoid, delusional, and potentially suicidal off on his own, unsupervised and unattended. She acknowledged that it probably wasn't. Then she confided in hushed tones that it was too bad, really, but since the last round of cutbacks, there just wasn't good care to be found for psychiatric patients.

Not finding this observation reassuring, I went looking to determine whether there was anything I could do to get Liv out of emergency and into the psychiatric unit.

I WAS GIVEN A PHYSICAL BY
A NURSE WHO ASKED IF
I WORKED. I SAID I DID
BUT I DID NOT SAY IT
WAS VOLUNTEER WORK.

MOM BROUGHT MY
OVERNIGHT SUITCASE

Since my brother's psychiatrist was now out of town, I called a psychiatrist acquaintance. Could she share any information or provide me with some connections that might assist Olivier? "No," she answered regretfully. She had heard that waiting times for psychiatric patients could be extensive—there was, as usual, a city-wide bed shortage—but gave me the number of the person coordinating schizophrenic care at the Regional Health Authority.

I phoned, made an appointment, and met with this regional representative at his office. I explained the situation to him: that as of Day Three my brother was still perched, untreated, unsupervised, in a hallway. I told him I was worried.

He took notes and was sympathetic but told me that a long wait wasn't unusual for psychiatric patients. Sometimes it extended to five days, even in emergencies.

So, I asked, was there *anything* I could do to speed up the process? He looked something up in a book, wrote down an address, and handed it to me. The prescription he offered was that I should write a letter of concern to the premier of our province.

And so it went. No one was responsible, or everyone was responsible, and there was never anything to be done in any case.

Eventually, at the end of the third day, my brother was finally admitted and a bed was found for him in the psychiatric unit.

But if the motto of the medical health profession is "First, do no harm," I would suggest that leaving someone experiencing a mental health crisis in a hallway, unsupervised for days, holds potential for enormous harm.

I'd argue that individuals with mental health issues currently receive second-class care in our health care system, and that there are not just cracks in the mental health system, but gaping chasms that people with mental health problems drop through on a regular basis.

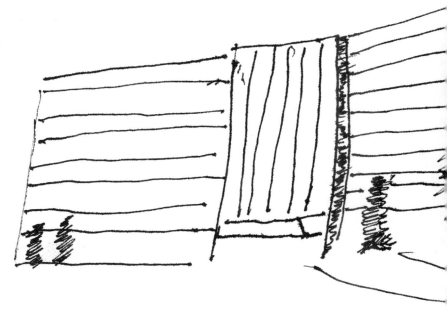

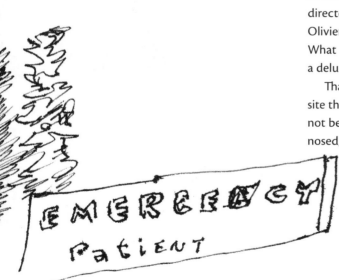

The long queues for beds are just one symptom of that problem—after all, my brother had been directed by his doctor to go to the hospital, and Olivier was agreeable about accepting treatment. What happens to the family in crisis that brings a delusional relative in who is afraid or suspicious?

That individual will surely not wait the requisite three, four, or five days and consequently will not be seen by a psychiatrist, will not be diagnosed, will not receive treatment.

Liv remained in the hospital for a number of weeks as his doctors consulted about how to proceed.

This was the dilemma, though. Liv had, by this point, more or less tried the majority of the antipsychotics. In each case they either were ineffective or led to crippling side effects. For a period of time, he was put back on a combination of Risperdal and Luvox, but that didn't solve the essential problem.

Shortly after this episode, Liv was referred to another psychiatrist. His new consulting psychiatrist considered the track record of the previously administered drugs and noted that there was one other option that hadn't been explored.

I'd already heard of clozapine.

There was a wealth of existing literature touting its effectiveness. Some people referred to it as the "Cadillac of antipsychotics," both because of its high success rate for managing the symptoms of schizophrenia and its prohibitively high price tag.

But unlike other drugs, the risks associated with clozapine were so severe that you first had to qualify as a candidate just to receive a prescription. The drug had a major drawback. In a phenomenon known as agranulocytosis, a significant proportion of candidates taking the drug found their white blood cells attacked. This is a potentially fatal condition.

Because of the danger associated with agranulocytosis, clozapine is reserved for patients with schizophrenia who have either failed to respond to all other antipsychotic drugs or present as particularly suicidal.

There was a special procedure applied in the transition to clozapine. Patients were required to stay in a hospital where blood samples could be monitored for a period of four weeks to ensure that the white blood cell count didn't drop to dangerous levels.

Clozapine presented another complication. Patients taking it often gained a significant amount of weight. Liv had already put on considerable weight during his previous drug regimen and was, following his treatment with olanzapine, classified as a diabetic.

Liv held a consultation with his psychiatrist and returned home with this message. Before he could be assessed as a candidate for clozapine, he would have to shed thirty pounds. His psychiatrist would assess his results in three months' time to see what he'd achieved.

DOCTOR I WOULD LIKE
TO TRY CLOZAPINE

YOU'RE DIABETIC
SO YOU'LL HAVE TO
LOSE 30 POUNDS
WE DON'T WANT TO
HAVE HYPERGLYCEMIA

I WENT FOR WALKS
WITH MY NURSE BARBARA

Liv was eager to do something and so took the advice to heart. He set up a program that he could follow and did all the right things. He ate smaller portions at meal times. Snacked less often. He walked regularly.

After a month, he stepped on the scale to find he'd lost three pounds.

I WALKED EARLY IN THE MORNING AND LATE AT NIGHT

I MET MY BROTHER
IN THE HALLWAY. MOM
MADE TEA FOR HIM.

WE ATE SEMOLINA
AND DRANK TEA AND
COFFEE.

I WALKED HIM OUT TO
HIS BUICK CENTURY.

The family convened and agreed that we'd have to coordinate a more organized approach.

I suggested that a concrete destination might be a good idea when Liv went for a walk. That way it wouldn't just be a walk—it would be a walk *to* somewhere. That would make things more interesting. Liv's response was that it would only make things interesting if the destination was interesting.

He could, I offered, walk to my house. It was a longer hike and would take him forty-five minutes to an hour, but once there, I could provide him with non-caloric mint tea as refreshment. And then I could drive him back home after.

Nic responded with the suggestion that Liv and he could go out on a regular series of outdoor wilderness activities: hiking or snowshoeing.

That became the template for the new, more vigorous exercise agenda. Liv walked each morning on his own. He hiked to my house later in the afternoon for mint tea. On weekends he accompanied Nic on various mountain paths.

I COLLECTED THE RECYCLING BOTTLES TO TAKE TO THE BOTTLE DEPOT

I DECIDED TO WALK TO THE DEPOT.

I WAITED IN LINE TO GIVE MY BOTTLES.

I EMPTIED MY BOTTLES

I RECEIVED $1.25

I WALKED BACK HOME

I WENT FOR A WALK FOR FORTY FIVE MINUTES

Liv dropped another ten pounds and then plateaued. No amount of activity or change of diet or wishful thinking seemed able to alter his weight.

It was frustrating. We knew from our reading that the antipsychotics appeared to alter the metabolism in some individuals. Still, Liv seemed to be doing everything he could.

If he didn't shed the weight, however, then he wouldn't convince his doctor to place him on the list. If he couldn't be placed on the list, he couldn't access the clozapine—and then what options would he have? The deadline was only a month away.

SHE MEASURED MY WAIST

The pitch of activity escalated. My mother stormed about the kitchen, consulting new Weight Watchers cookbooks in her preparation of low-fat meals. Liv consumed fresh fruit snacks at lunch. He joined the Canadian Mental Health Association's walking club. He began drinking large amounts of water. This was supposed to hold some kind of special caloric benefit.

(I'm not sure how *that* is supposed to work, really. The idea is that if you drink water, you quench your thirst and so your craving for something, and you feel more full. I just find that I have to go to the washroom more often, and am still as hungry as ever.)

The deadline arrived. Liv nervously drove to his appointment. His psychiatrist administered his checkup and told him pretty much what we'd all expected. He was still twelve pounds over.

But she didn't entirely rule out the possibility that he might still receive clozapine. She said she'd give him another three months to continue trying. If he couldn't drop sufficient weight by the end of that time, though, she would move on to another applicant.

I met Liv at the condominium and he told me what the doctor had said. He was disheartened and I could tell he was thinking through the implications. What would his life be like if he couldn't find something that would produce fewer side effects?

I said that it was too bad, but that he still had another three months.

"Oh well," he replied.

"Oh well what?"

"Just, oh well."

I WANTED TO GO ON A HIKE. I KNEW I WAS TO BRING WATER AND A LUNCH

THE DRIVER LAWRENCE AND VICTOR WERE THERE

The news set him back for a few days, but he didn't give up. Over the next three months he continued dieting and exercising. He continued to meet regularly with the walking club at the CMHA, and the therapist coordinating that group was very encouraging.

From time to time I would walk with him. We would discuss a variety of subjects as we ambled, and I found the hikes enjoyable in a way I hadn't anticipated. Walking was something we'd done a lot as youngsters. It was what you did when you didn't have sufficient money to do anything more interesting.

And, of course, my father had been a prodigious stroller. He'd walked everywhere, partially because of his obsessive thrift, but also because he genuinely relished walking. He used to tell me that was how he thought best. He would "walk an idea."

I remembered reading a story when I was young, about the sun and the wind having an argument. They couldn't agree who was more powerful and so determined to hold a contest. The first to compel this one man—a poor soul innocently out minding his own business—to take off his jacket would win.

The wind started. It blew and blew, but the man pulled his clothes tighter about him and kept his jacket firmly on. The sun took its turn. It radiated beneficently, and eventually the man, growing too warm, relented and peeled off his outer layers. In this story, the sun triumphed.

My father, to me, had always been that man. When I considered the story I imagined that in the primitively rendered illustrations, it was my father leaning grimly into the wind. And later in the story as the hot sunlight beamed down, it was he who removed his coat.

Now, as Liv and I walked, the sun warmed *us*, and we shed our jackets.

Although I recognized that we were exercising as part of a weight-loss regimen and that there were specific goals that Liv was trying to attain, part of me felt transported by this routine. We had somehow been conveyed to another, simpler, time before schizophrenia and before drug treatments, when there had been nothing more complicated than deciding where to place your jacket once you had removed it.

THE PETER LOUGHEED
WILL PHONE YOU WHEN
THEY HAVE A SPACE
YOU MUST BE READY
TO GO IMMEDIATELY

The next deadline approached and Liv attended his consultation again. He stepped onto the scale and found he was still five pounds over.

It's possible that his psychiatrist had set the goal higher than she needed. Maybe she thought Liv required that kind of motivation, that it would spur him to greater efforts. In any case, she told him that even though he was a little over the limit, he could stop worrying. She would send his application forward.

A week later, Liv's application was accepted.

He was directed to check into the hospital to perform the transition to clozapine. It would take about a month, and during that time his blood would be monitored on a daily basis.

The family experienced mixed feelings. After all, there was no guarantee that this drug would be any more effective than the others. We knew that. We knew that Liv might transition to clozapine and then discover that his side effects carried on unabated. And we knew that if he experienced any trouble with his white cell count during the transition, the clozapine would be discontinued, and he would be right back where he started.

Still, after all the work and effort Liv had put into reducing his weight and getting his application processed, we couldn't help feeling both happy for him and a little triumphant. Personally, I felt like the small-town amateur coach of a suddenly very successful Olympic athlete.

WHEN I SCRATCHED ON
THE EIGHT BALL TWICE
AND LOST TWO GAMES
BECKY SAID "HOW MANY FINGERS
DO YOU SEE?" ALL I COULD
DO WAS NOD MY HEAD AND
SAY "YOU'RE RIGHT."

GORD BECKY AND I
HEADED TOWARD THE
C TRAIN. LINDA HAD SOME
SHOPPING TO DO.

AS I WAS LOOKING AT BATIKS
I SAW BECKY. SHE WAS LOOKING
AT SOME CLOTHES. SHE SAID
"I WAS TRYING TO PICK HER UP."
I LAUGHED.

Liv stayed in the hospital for several weeks, and during that time his blood levels remained good. I was caught off guard by how well he adapted to hospital life. I realized, with a bit of a start, just how much of his time over the years he had spent at hospitals. He knew what was expected of him, where everything was located, and how to talk to the clients and the caregivers.

Still, four weeks in a hospital is a long stay. Even if you know your way around the psychiatric unit, it will wear on you. There can be a lot of activity at night and, depending on who has checked in at the time, a lot of drama. He began to look forward to being released. At last, it appeared that the drug was going to have no impact upon his white blood cells, and he was permitted a temporary pass to go home for the weekend.

LIFE ON THE UNIT WAS THE SAME. SOME
PEOPLE PACING FOR MILES SOME PEOPLE
TALKING ON THE PHONE

But the results of his most recent test still had to be confirmed before he would be given his weekend pass. When the tests finally arrived on the unit, the regular staff had finished their shift. It was the night-duty nurse who Liv had to sign off with.

I waited farther down the hallway and watched as Liv approached her. She was obviously tired. She searched for notes regarding his release but couldn't lay her hands on them. She told him that he could sign out for the two days but didn't offer him any medication to take during his absence.

Liv hesitated, then reminded her that his doctor had told him he would be given a prescription to take home.

The nurse shrugged. "There's nothing like that indicated here," she said, pointing at the log book.

"But I came here to transition onto—" he started again, but she cut him off.

"Nothing's been left for you."

"But—"

"It'll *only* be for the weekend."

I flinched at the tone she employed. It was the dismissive tone that you might have used with a—I'm not sure who you could have used it with, actually. It was the tone you would use if you thought someone was particularly slow. The power disparity in that exchange was striking. It was clear that she didn't think my brother could possibly have anything to tell her that could inform her decision or change her mind. Liv returned to where I was waiting.

"Should *I* talk to her?" I asked quietly.

He gave a quick shake of his head. "No," he said. "It won't do any good with her. Let's just go."

And he was right; it wouldn't have done any good. I would have been seen as interfering. It would have been framed as an invasion of patient confidentiality. It would have done nothing.

So, I drove him home.

But only two hours after I'd dropped him off, he received a phone call from another person at the hospital, telling him that the instructions he'd received were wrong. There *were* drugs he had to take. In fact, it would be dangerous if he *didn't* take his medication.

He was instructed to return to the hospital immediately to pick them up.

It made for a weird ending to what was, otherwise, a successful transition.

And that, for me, captures precisely the problem presented by the continued downloading of responsibility of care. Although more and more accountability is delivered to patients and their families, it's not guided by shared information or framed by genuine dialogue.

After I returned home and thought about the incident with the nurse, I felt like I should have intervened, that I hadn't done enough, that if Liv had become sick on his weekend visit it would have been partially because I had failed. But the fact is that while families are expected to offer assistance, they aren't invited to question the standards of treatment or to intervene.

Following that weekend release, it was determined that Liv was responding well and he was discharged from the hospital.

Clozapine wasn't the instant success we might have hoped for. For several months after Liv was released, he appeared tired and disoriented. But none of the previous disabling side effects ever recurred.

In the end, the medication proved more successful than we could have imagined. Over time Liv's energy picked up and his thinking grew clearer. He became more optimistic.

He had been so anxious, so depressed for so long that I'd begun to think of that as normal. As his depression faded, I began to remember another side of him. He started to smile again—which may seem like a banal observation, but it had been a very long time since I'd really seen him smile. It was, without exaggerating, a sea change in his personality.

Years after he began this treatment, he's remained in good spirits and the best state of mind I've seen him exhibit in more than twenty years.

And he has maintained the exercise regime that he initiated while preparing to get tested, so he continues walking. That has to be considered a positive result as well.

I've noticed that for whatever reasons, whenever Liv draws me, I end up looking like one of those mad and bad scientists in science fiction films from the Sixties—bald, stern, and possessing a gleaming expanse of forehead.

I'd characterize the relationship I have with Liv as both good and close, but there are times when I know I get on his nerves. I ask too many questions. I take things seriously that are only suggested ironically. I offer too much unsolicited advice. His obsessions and anxieties don't always receive a sympathetic ear from me, and maybe I could be more relaxed or should be more sympathetic. This is partially because there is an element of me that can be cussed and demanding; partially it is a result of the influence the illness has had on us. Over time schizophrenia disassembles and reconstructs all lines of communication.

Sometimes he tells me that I don't understand the way things are. And I'm certain that sometimes he's right. How could I? He's lived an experience that I have only observed.

And ultimately, when I was younger and had mapped out our lives I was certainly wrong.

I didn't know maps well enough. I didn't understand how flawed an instrument they could be, how difficult to manage, how impossible it was to cast the currents of chance and choice.

I never developed my anticipated career at a zoo. By some strange twist of fate, Nic, though he still seems most completely at home in the woods threading a canoe through swift channels and streams, became first a software programmer and then a manager of other software programmers. Ben left the map so much earlier than I could possibly have imagined. And life has drawn a completely different path for Liv.

Since then, I've learned other things. I've come to understand that schizophrenia takes things. It seizes people. It confiscates relationships. It snatches peace of mind and slips it away in some deep, secret, interior pocket.

It takes so much, in fact, that at times it seems insatiable. It seems it will consume everything.

Only later do you discover that schizophrenia gives things back too. Not all that it took, and not all at once. It returns them late. They seem unrecognizable at first, gone as long as they've been, but slowly you begin to recall them.

Over the years I've seen Liv returning. He's not the person I knew when I was younger, but in many ways he's returned stronger, more resilient. I have become aware of how genuinely patient he is with people. How generous he is with his time when he volunteers, how forgiving he is of others' foibles. How kind and devoted an uncle.

It's the middle of winter as I write this. We've been working, Liv and I, on the book. We're walking back to his place, talking things over as we go. Between our snatches of conversation he hums in that quiet, curiously high-pitched and ever so slightly off-key fashion that he has. Since the humming renders it pretty much incomprehensible, I'm unable to immediately match title to tune. Then I catch one line and realize with some astonishment that it's Bruce Springsteen's "Dancing in the Dark." "'You can't start a fire,'" Liv warbles. "'Can't start a fire without a spark, this gun's for hire. Even if we're just dancing in the dark.'"

And it may only be because I'm already in a positive frame of mind, but the song strikes me a certain way. I feel curiously buoyant. I recollect how completely in the dark we've felt at times and how that doesn't seem to hold true anymore.

The snow squeaks under the heavy tread of our boots. I am aware that although we are taking strides of different lengths, we are somehow walking together.

Epilogue

My brother and mother still share a place. Ten years ago they decided they had to move. The grey stuccoed home where we grew up hemorrhaged old memories, and, as small as it was, it proved too much house for them to manage. Where the lawn wasn't burnt brown from under-watering, it grew in swaying, uncut thickets. Inside the house, things gathered. Magazines accumulated in teetering stacks. The shelves above the coat rack strained under the weight of hats from every possible historical period of hat development.

Clutter began to take over and hedge Mom and Liv in. Finally, they relocated to a condominium, where they have lived together since, providing equal measures of support, encouragement, and irritation for each other.

Over their many years together, Liv and my
mother have developed their complementary
strengths. My mother's eyesight is bad, so she
doesn't drive much anymore. My brother deals
with the car instead. My brother is a relentless
gatherer, throwing nothing away. My mother is
a whirlwind of disposal, organizing and thrusting
all matter into the recycling box, the newspaper
bag, or the garbage bin.

When my mother's hip gave out, Liv helped
her get up and about until she could get an
implant. After Liv's diabetic attack, my mother
ensured he took his daily tests.

They offer a kind of support that can't be
found anywhere else, and occasionally they drive
each other around the bend.

But being part of a family isn't enough.

Although the focus of this book has been on our family's experience, it's impossible to receive everything you require within a single household. Over the decades, Liv has cautiously developed an intricate, extended network that offers him guidance and support. Much of that network is connected to the not-for-profits that operate from inner-city locations.

Scan the fabric of each major city in North America and you will discover a similar development. And if you look carefully, you will realize the institutionalization that was the norm in the 1960s hasn't disappeared. It has only been outsourced on a diminished budget.

The mental health ghetto sprawls. It's made up of a network that exists primarily within the core of major cities across the continent, but the geography alters slightly according to the season, and the transience of the population—and it has permeable boundaries. Some people are connected through the support groups they attend. Many people with mental illness are on government assistance and live in subsidized housing. A significant number live on the streets. And within the various segments, there is movement, flux, and change. Individuals return to homes occasionally, or return to hospitals, or sometimes return to prison.

It's worth reflecting a moment upon the significance of the imprisoned population because it represents a considerable demographic. A recent study indicated that the number of people in American jails with mental illness has grown so drastically over the past decades that the U.S. prison system now constitutes the single-largest mental health care provider in America.

The situation in Canada is little better. In a recent interview about the increasing number of psychiatric patients in prisons across the country, Val Villeneuve, director of forensic psychiatry services in Southern Alberta, offered: "What we're seeing is the criminalization of the mentally ill."

Which only confirmed comments made by the Coalition for Appropriate Care and Treatment—a Canadian mental health lobby group—about trends in North America.

I FEAR BEING IN JAIL

"In some jurisdictions more than 95% of beds for treating mental illness in provincial or state hospitals have closed. While the reasons are contentious, few disagree that deinstitutionalization has been a major policy failure.... In part this failure is the result of a reluctance to pay for the services needed to provide treatment and support in the community. But there has also been a failure to recognize the extent of the functional deficits caused by serious mental illness and a consequent failure to provide appropriate types of services to prevent people from relapsing. The result is that many individuals run foul of the law—often because of minor crimes. With so few hospital beds available to provide secure treatment these individuals end up in jail."

Everyone who is part of the mental health community knows someone who has spent time in prison. And it becomes, for them, a kind of cautionary tale. It's what keeps them silent. It's what ensures that they don't complain. They know what can happen if things go awry with their treatment.

The mental health ghetto exists, like any ghetto exists, because it serves the dominant culture's desire to segregate a group and it simultaneously fills critical needs of that particular client community.

My brother has friends he sees regularly who are part of that community. And he has access to clinics and services, and receives a kind of understanding within the ghetto that he can't get elsewhere.

He plays pool with one group that meets weekly in the inner city. He slips past panhandlers to attend art classes at Self-Help, where he sketches and sculpts. A few blocks over, Opportunity Works offers counselling, and on Thursdays he meets with the Circle of Friends at the Canadian Mental Health Association. He moves in and out, meeting with his peers because they understand his situation in a way that the rest of society—including my family and me—often don't.

These organizations all survive on the thinnest of margins. After Liv's art class failed to receive government funding one year, it was cancelled. The following year a fundraiser attracted interest from a sponsor and rescued the program. The vagaries of the economy have serious consequences for the sustainability of the smaller agencies, and financial support remains unreliable. And of course, these agencies are all overwhelmed by the multiple needs presented by their homeless clientele.

I remember a rather sad conversation I had with a colleague a while back; she also had a brother with schizophrenia, about the same age as Liv. She told me how difficult it had been for her to provide care for her brother, how helpless she had felt. Delusional and paranoid, he had grown suspicious of treatment. Increasingly he struggled at the edges of society. She tried to maintain contact, but it's a big city. One day he simply vanished. No one knew where he'd gone. She spent years trying to find him, but he never turned up. She didn't know for certain whether he was alive or dead, although she felt it was more likely the latter.

I GET TO SELF HELP
USUALLY AT 8:30 AM

I WAIT UNTIL 9:00 AM
TO GO TO MY ART CLASS

MARLENE MAKES COFFEE WITH
SUSAN AND MELISSA

I SAID GOODBYE
TO MARLENE

I SAW TWO MEN FIGHTING
AND YELLING AND
SPILLING SOME RED DRINK

I WENT TO THE
CORNER TO CROSS
THE STREET

The system is a mess. Two-thirds of those with mental illness never receive treatment. Families lack the assistance, guidance, and training required to respond to the kinds of situations they encounter. Mental illness is mostly misunderstood by the public, and critical issues of mental illness are mishandled at nearly every level of the health care system. What's to be done?

To start with, those in the highest levels of our health care system must stop shutting their eyes, pretending that nothing is wrong, pretending that psychiatric services are receiving adequate support. They're not. Above all, both federal and provincial governments must finally demonstrate leadership and behave in a manner that communicates to the public that mental illness isn't a lapse of character, isn't a product of degenerate morality, isn't something that if swept onto our streets or concealed behind bars will simply disappear. It hasn't, it won't, and we all deserve better.

I MET A GUY NAMED STEPHEN
I HAVE MET HIM BEFORE
AT SELF HELP

HE ASKED ME IF I HAD SEEN
ANY ONE WHO WAS PERFECT.

I SAID "NO I NEVER HAD."
"MAYBE IN OUR MINDS PEOPLE
ARE PERFECT."

the end

Acknowledgements

A number of individuals and organizations deserve acknowledgement for their efforts. Melanie Little, Sarah Ivany, Robyn Read, and Natalie Olsen for the passion and vision they have demonstrated throughout the development of this book. For their assistance and support, Peter Norman, Jackie Flanagan, the Calgary Association of Self Help, the Canadian Mental Health Association, and the entire Martini tribe. Dr. Donald Addington's thoughtful input was generously offered and gratefully accepted. And Chandra, Miranda, and Cheryl—many thanks for the very welcome, carefully worded, and always insightful observations.

Notes

Part One

Page 47: Government of Canada, *The Human Face of Mental Health and Mental Illness in Canada* 2006 (Ottawa, Ontario: Minister of Public Works and Government Services Canada, 2006), 74.

Part Six

Page 159: Roy Romanow, *Building on Values: The Future of Health Care in Canada* (Ottawa, Ontario: Commission on the Future of Health Care in Canada, 2002), 178.

Page 162: Marilyn Ellas, "Mentally Ill Die 25 Years Earlier, on Average," *USA Today* (May 3, 2007).

Page 163: Kate Torgovnick, "Why Do the Mentally Ill Die Younger?" *TIME* (December 3, 2008).

Page 163: Conference Board of Canada, "Mortality Due to Mental Disorders," www.conferenceboard.ca, September 2009.

Page 165: Ellas, "Mentally Ill Die 25 Years Earlier."

Page 165: Torgovnick, "Why Do the Mentally Ill Die Younger?"

Part Seven

Page 193: Alex Berenson, "One Drug, Two Faces," *The New York Times* (March 26, 2008).

Part Eight

Page 252: Government of Canada, *Human Face of Mental Health*, 74.

Page 252: Jamie Fellner, "A Corrections Quandary, Mental Illness and Prison Rules," *Harvard Civil Rights–Civil Liberties Law Review* 41 (Summer 2006).

Page 252: Dawn Walton, "The Mad and the Bad," *The Globe and Mail* (June 26, 2008).

Page 253: The Coalition for Appropriate Care and Treatment (CFACT), "The Criminalization of People Who Suffer from Serious Mental Illness," www.cfact.ca/criminalization.asp.

Page 259: Rena Scheffer, *Addressing Stigma: Increasing Public Understanding of Mental Illness* (Toronto, Ontario: Centre for Addiction and Mental Health, May 28, 2003).

Additional Sources

Canadian Institute for Health Information. *Improving the Health of Canadians: Mental Health, Delinquency and Criminal Activity*. Ottawa, Ontario: CIHI, 2008.

Forensic Mental Health Services, Expert Advisory Panel. *Assessment, Treatment and Community Reintegration of the Mentally Disordered Offender*. Toronto, Ontario: Ontario Ministry of Health and Long-Term Care, 2002.

Kirby, the Honourable Michael J.L., chair. *Out of the Shadows at Last: Transforming Mental Illness*. Ottawa, Ontario: Standing Senate Committee on Social Affairs, Science and Technology, 2006.

Marshall, Jamie. *Mental Health and Addictions Populations*. Kelowna, British Columbia: Official Community Plan. Mental Health and Addictions, Okanagan Health Service Area, 2009.

Riordan, Tim. *Exploring the Circle: Mental Illness, Homelessness and the Criminal Justice System in Canada*. Ottawa, Ontario: Government of Canada, Political and Social Affairs Division, 2004.